Primroses and Auriculas

D1332218

RHS WISLEY HANDBOOKS

Primroses and Auriculas

Peter Ward

MITCHELL BEAZLEY

THE ROYAL HORTICULTURAL SOCIETY

Primroses and Auriculas
Peter Ward

First published in Great Britain in 2003 by Cassell Illustrated, an imprint
of Octopus Publishing Group Limited.
This edition published in 2008 in association with the Royal
Horticultural Society by Mitchell Beazley, an imprint of Octopus
Publishing Group Limited, 2–4 Heron Quays, London E14 4JP
An Hachette Livre UK Company
www.octopusbooks.co.uk

Copyright © Octopus Publishing Group 2008
Text copyright © Peter Ward 2008

All rights reserved. No part of this work may be reproduced or utilized
in any form or by any means, electronic or mechanical, including
photocopying, recording or by any information storage and retrieval
system, without the prior written permission of the publisher.

The publishers will be grateful for any information that will assist them
in keeping future editions up to date. Although all reasonable care has
been taken in the preparation of this book, neither the publishers nor
the author can accept any liability for any consequence arising from the
use thereof, or the information contained therein.

The author has asserted his moral rights.

A CIP catalogue record for this book is available from the
British Library.

ISBN 978 1 84533 385 0

Commissioning Editor Camilla Stoddart
Designer Justin Hunt

Set in Bembo

Colour reproduction by Dot Gradations Ltd.
Printed and bound by Toppan in China

CONTENTS

*'Nickity' – a
peach-edged
show auricula*

THE PRIMROSES

The genus *Primula* is one of the largest in cultivation in temperate gardens and includes over 400 species, of which the majority are confined to the Himalayas and western China. Europe has only 33 species, mostly in the Alps, with five native to the British Isles. The species are classified into many botanical sections, only two of which are covered in this book: primroses are part of section *Primula*, and auriculas are part of section *Auricula*.

Primroses form a relatively small section that includes the polyanthus primulas and the British native primrose (*P. vulgaris*), cowslip (*P. veris*) and oxlip (*P. elatior*). These three British natives, along with the two foreign *P. vulgaris* subspecies *sibthorpii* and *heterochroma*, and the diminutive *P. juliae* from the eastern half of the Caucasus, are the parents of a multitude of hybrid primroses and polyanthus now grown extensively throughout Europe, North America and Australasia. Two other little-known species, *P. megaseifolia* and *P. renifolia*, are included in section *Primula*, but so far have made little contribution in terms of new hybrids.

Primroses take their name from the Latin name for cowslips and primroses, *Primula veris* meaning 'the first little thing of spring'. Coloured forms of the primrose were introduced from Europe and the Near East, and they were grown in the gardens of the wealthy. They interbred with our native yellow *P. vulgaris* and the best of the seedlings were distributed, often under a clonal name. During the late 17th and early 18th centuries the gold-laced polyanthus appeared, followed later in the 18th century by the predecessor of the garden polyanthus, believed to be a hybrid between the primrose and the cowslip.

Primula vulgaris

6

Double primroses – mutations of the single primrose – were discovered growing in the wild and transferred to gardens. Different colours appeared, as well as anomalous or unusual forms. All arose as chance seedlings or were the result of placing plants together and allowing nature to do its work.

In 1900 Julia Mlokossjewicz discovered *P. juliae* and plants or seed were sent to England. Soon hundreds of new hybrids were appearing, crosses with our native species. In the late 18th century the garden polyanthus was also being developed, initially by Gertude Jekyll who produced the Munstead strain of whites and yellows. From these humble beginnings, dozens of strains eventually resulted in a range of brilliant colours on large robust plants.

Today primroses and polyanthus, far removed in appearance from the original species, are part of a huge commercial industry, and millions are sold annually, both as pot plants and for the garden. The more traditional sorts are still grown, primarily by enthusiasts.

PRIMROSE SPECIES

Primula vulgaris, our native primrose, often known as *P. acaulis*, and *P. veris*, the cowslip, are among our best-loved plants. Once known as 'Vernales' primulas, primroses and cowslips, along with *P. elatior*, the oxlip, are now considered to be part of section Primula of subgenus primula. Some disagreement about the exact classification exists among botanists but is not of great relevance to gardeners.

Primula vulgaris

Preferring the broken shade of open deciduous woodland, primroses are often also seen on sites that offer similar conditions, such as north-facing slopes and sheltered banks. They will grow on a range of soils, from heavy and slightly acid to limey, but dislike peaty and waterlogged sites and very light, dry soils. They are widely distributed throughout much of the British Isles and Ireland, mostly in areas where broad-leaved woodland is well-established. Once abundant, their numbers declined through the 20th century until 1975, when the taking of plants from the wild became illegal. This ban, together with deliberate amenity planting, has seen populations increasing and

Primula vulgaris

they now flourish on motorway banks, railway embankments and similar sites, as well as in more natural habitats. In Cornwall they flower as early as February, in Scotland as late as June.

The present British population is largely yellow-flowered. White forms are sometimes found and also some in pink or pale reddish shades. The latter are widely thought to be hybrids with garden primroses, although some experts argue that they may be true wild species. As well as the normal yellow, among the subspecies that grow abroad are white-flowered forms and others in shades of pink, purple, red, and violet. Old gardening magazines and *floras* contain numerous reports of wild primroses in many colours other than yellow. Such colour variations are no longer in existence.

Primula veris

Cowslips are well known throughout Europe and their range extends almost to the Pacific Coast. It is evident from the literature in existence that they have been considered important for many

centuries. They prefer more open sites than primroses, growing in well-drained, neutral soil on grassy fields or banks, also light woodland, up to 3000m (9000ft). Once common in much of England, less so in Scotland, Ireland and Wales, habitat destruction and intensive farming in the 20th century devastated their numbers. Large quantities were also picked, not least for their wine-making qualities. Fortunately, as with the primrose, legal protection and amenity planting has reversed this trend. There are four subspecies.

Primula veris

Primula elatior

Primula elatior

The oxlip is the least known of the trio and has a very restricted range in the British Isles, being principally found in East Anglia and centred around the borders of Cambridge, Essex and Suffolk: in other localities hybrids between the primrose and cowslip, known as 'false oxlips', masquerade as oxlips.

Again, habitat destruction has reduced its numbers but where it grows, the oxlip is locally abundant and may be increasing. Its preferred habitat is broad-leaved woodland, usually oak, on wet, chalky clay soils. There are several subspecies growing in parts of Europe and beyond. Some are very choice plants, including *P. elatior* subsp. *meyeri*, often incorrectly called *P. amoena*, which has flowers in lovely shades of violet-blue through lavender to purple.

Primula juliae

P. juliae was discovered by Julia Ludvikovna Mlokossjewicz, daughter of a Polish aristocrat and botanist, at Lagodekh in the eastern Caucasus on 20 April, 1900, growing in moss among wet and dripping rocks, close to waterfalls. It makes large carpets of creeping rhizomes with fleshy reddish scales forming close to the ground. The stalked flowers are bright, deep bluish-magenta, darker and redder round the yellow eye. White forms are said to exist.

Primula juliae

An easy grower in damp, shaded conditions, *P. juliae* does well in pots, although it is not free-flowering in cultivation, and poor forms abound. The date of introduction to Britain is disputed, with most sources saying the species was sent to Kew and Oxford in 1911 by Professor Kusnetsow of Dorpat Botanical Gardens. However, the famous nurseryman Clarence Elliot wrote that Mr Baker of Oxford Botanic Gardens obtained seeds from Tiflis Botanical Garden in 1911. On 2 April 1912 Baker exhibited *P. juliae* at the Royal Horticultural Society and the plant was given an Award of Merit.

Although overshadowed by the large-flowered hybrids, the primrose species, especially some of the subspecies, are well worth growing. They include some very choice plants and have considerable potential for hybridizing.

TYPES OF PRIMROSE AND POLYANTHUS

Single Primroses

Primroses became popular garden plants towards the end of the 15th century. They were abundant in the wild and were collected for medicinal and sweetening purposes. The early herbals, not strictly gardening books, were concerned

Gemini mixed

with plants of medicinal value and these contain the earliest references to the cultivation of cowslips and primroses.

In 1640 the king's botanist, John Parkinson described 'Tradescants Turkie-Purple Primrose' (thought to be *P. vulgaris* subsp. *sibthorpii*) which John Tradescant brought back from the coast of the Black Sea. By 1648 Jason Bobart the elder was growing blue, purple and white forms at Oxford Botanic Garden, as well as the 'feild primerose'. John Rea provided the first information about coloured varieties of primroses in 1665. He listed more than 20 shades, all 'diversities of red', and implied they came from abroad.

From the 17th century until the early 1900s many coloured forms of primrose were grown in gardens. They were either selected, seed collected from different plants growing together, or chance seedlings. Up to this time hand-pollination was not practised, although it was well understood, and line breeding was unknown. Reports on the 1903 and 1904 RHS Shows record the 'marvellous Primula hybrids from elatior [and] vulgaris' that were exhibited. These coloured forms became collectors' items, although never achieving the status of the double and anomalous forms.

The new primroses (18th and 19th centuries), which

occurred in shades of red, purple, blue and lilac were found to be less hardy than the native wild plants. Named varieties were rare, one such being 'Oakwood Blue', raised by G.H. Wilson. It was given the RHS Award of Merit in 1890 and was described as a 'deep indigo blue – best yet'. Also by the end of the 19th century nurserymen were working on improved strains that could be raised from seed.

The introduction of *P. juliae* in 1911 brought about a revolution in primrose breeding. Plant breeders throughout Europe – amateurs as well as professionals – crossed *P. juliae* with the various primroses and cowslips and many hybrids were soon being introduced. The most famous of these is 'Wanda', which was raised by Bakers of Wolverhampton and given the RHS Award of Merit on 8 April 1919. However, despite frequent claims to the contrary, this was not the first *P. juliae* hybrid, its seed parent being a 'crimson form of *P. acaulis*'. 'Crispii', raised by Waterer Sons and Crisp, received the Award of Merit in 1916. It was the result of a cross between *P. juliae* and the 'common primrose'.

Over the next 50 years, many hundreds of hybrids between primroses and *P. juliae* were introduced in England, Ireland and the continent. It became something of a craze with several specialist nurseries issuing lists exceeding 100 named plants. Unfortunately the history of these varieties is vague with little valuable information available, often all that still exists is a name and a vague colour description. In North America hybridization work did not begin until the 1930s, the initiators being Florence Bellis in Oregon and William Goddard in

Forza

Vancouver. Unlike their British counterparts, many of these North American *P. juliae* hybrids still survive.

As well as being the home of a number of *P. juliae* hybrids, Ireland is also the origin of the interesting 'Garryard' primroses, which were mostly of mixed primrose/polyanthus habit. They are descended from a sport of the wild primrose that arose in the garden of Mr Whiteside-Dane in County Kildare around 1900. Named 'Apple Blossom', this plant was distinguished by its bronze-coloured leaves, a feature that it bequeathed to all of its offspring, most of which also had pink and white flowers, although bronze-leaved plants with red flowers, and also white, were later introduced. 'Apple Blossom' is considered to have been either a mutation of *P. vulgaris* or a hybrid with a red primrose. One of the earliest and most famous of its offspring is 'Guinevere' (syn. 'Garryard Guinevere'), a plant that, through micropropagation, is commonly available today. Few, if any, of the other Garryards survive, although 'Enchantress', one of the best, may still grow in a few gardens.

The interest in primroses, especially *P. juliae* hybrids, remained strong until the late 1960s, when a rapid decline in availability of plants took place and most of the specialist nurseries closed. It has been said that viruses were the cause of the loss of so many of the named clones. The truth is more complex: seed strains, producing plants superior in many respects to the existing named plants, became available, while a run of hot, dry summers caused the loss of large numbers of plants, and, finally, changes in fashion, with many new 'novelties' being introduced, led to their decline.

The continued development of the primrose led to the large-flowered, gaudy plants we see today, which are not to everyone's taste. In turn, this has produced a revival in interest in the older sorts, with National Collections being established and some nurseries offering named clones. In America, the primrose remains popular and many named plants have been introduced, mainly by members of the American Primrose Society.

Double Primroses

The double primrose was first described by Tabernaemontanus in 1500. The early forms, surprisingly, seem to have been of polyanthus habit and were described by Clusius in 1601 as *P. veris vulgaris albo flore pleno*, a white double, and *P. veris vulgaris rubra flore pleno*, a shade of red.

Double cream seedling

Double primroses arose as sports of the single primrose and the double white and double lilac were common garden plants

from the mid-1600s to the mid-1930s. Many other doubles were reported as arising spontaneously from coloured forms of the single primrose growing in gardens. In the past, yellow, white, green and dull pink doubles have been discovered in the wild and are still occasionally found today. The history of the double-flowered primrose is much like that of the single-flowered primrose, with large numbers being raised by enthusiastic gardeners and nurserymen and ardently sought after by collectors. As with the single primrose, most have now

Double cerise seedling

disappeared; some old sorts still exist, but they are not up to the standard of the latest varieties. From time to time, 'double' seed became available but it often produced few, if any, double plants. All this changed in 1965, when Florence Bellis introduced the Barnhaven doubles at the April Coliseum Show in Portland, Oregon. Many doubles have been raised from this wonderful seed strain and double seed is still on offer from France, where Barnhaven is now located. Doubles have also been raised from seed of amateur hybridizers like Dr Cecil Jones of Llanelli, Wales, and Rosetta Jones of Shelton, Washington State. Lack of longevity, a major problem with the doubles, led to commercial micropropagation of a number of selected Barnhaven seedlings. These plants are sold annually through garden centres and some nurseries. A few amateur enthusiasts are also raising new seedlings, but the ongoing problem is the difficulty in maintaining selected clones, which tend to die out after two or three years.

Anomalous primroses

Anomalous – irregular, abnormal or deviation from the norm – describes mutations of the primrose and cowslip. They were popular during the Elizabethan period, which has led to them also being called 'Elizabethan' primroses, a more attractive term.

A tendency to mutate has occurred throughout the history of the primrose and cowslip. A 1614 florilegia by Crispin de Pas has two illustrations of unusual cowslip forms – a double and a hose-in-hose. Parkinson's famous *Paradisus Terrestris* of 1629 describes and illustrates 15 different types of primrose and six cowslips, both single and double, most of which can be classified as 'anomalous'. Various county *floras* mention anomalous forms, while old gardening magazines and RHS journals also provide further information.

The two most common anomalous forms are 'jack-in-the-greens' and 'hose-in-hose'. Several others are variations of or

Webster Yellow Jackanapes

Webster Laced hose-in-hose

even combinations of both these characteristics. They have names like 'Jackanapes', 'Pantaloons' and 'Galligaskins'. Jack-in-the-green describes plants with an enlarged calyx, a ruff of green leaves. They may be of either primrose or polyanthus form, single or double, and any colour. The green ruff varies in size, in its largest form, the individual flower seems to sit in the middle. Hose-in-hose flowers also come in both primrose and polyanthus forms. The calyx is petaloid giving the appearance of two identical flowers or corollas, one inside the other. At one time many named forms existed, but today most seen are seedlings; they are easy to raise since their unusual characteristics are dominant when crossed with other primroses.

In the last two or three years some astonishing new mutations have been exhibited by Margaret Webster at the annual exhibitions of the Midland and West and Southern sections of the National Primrose and Auricula Society (NAPS) (p.37). Most have been raised or collected by Margaret Webster and Dr Richard Brumpton of Nottingham, and while many are of scientific interest only, some are very attractive.

Gold-laced polyanthus

The gold-laced polyanthus is the only member of the primrose family that is classified as a florists' flower. This means it is grown to 'fixed and unalterable standards' and throughout its history has been closely associated with the florists' auricula.

Many growers and exhibitors of the show auricula also grew and exhibited gold-laced polyanthus. This still occurs today but not on the scale of past centuries. Initially known only as 'polyanthus', the term gold-laced was not commonly used until the latter half of the 19th century, when the need arose to differentiate between them and the newly introduced garden polyanthus. Apart from the lacing, the main difference between gold-laced and garden polyanthus is that the flowers are much smaller, varying between 1.5–2.5 cm ($^1/_2$–1 in). In addition, plants are smaller and less robust, but they are unusual and attractive plants for the garden and worth growing by non-specialists.

Gold-laced polyanthus were very popular in the first half of the 19th century, when hundreds of named varieties existed. They were widely exhibited and the best varieties changed hands at very high prices. After this, popularity declined and the plant, although still maintained by dedicated enthusiasts, suffered numerous crises. At one time it was claimed to be extinct in the British Isles and plants had to be re-introduced from America. The American plants were descendants of plants or seed obtained from Britain, and Florence Bellis of the Barnhaven Nursery made an important contribution.

Gold-laced polyanthus Danybanc Strain

Double gold-laced polyanthus

anomalous primroses

She sent seed to Britain and most British hybridizers have subsequently crossed Barnhaven plants with other British strains. However, as I have shown conclusively in my book *Primroses and Polyanthus* (B.T. Batsford, 1997), while scarce, the gold-laced polyanthus was never extinct in Britain.

It is worth noting that the strain of gold-laced raised by Lawrence Wigley, long-time secretary of the southern section of the NAPS, was given the much coveted Award of Garden Merit in the 1996–97 overwintering trial of polyanthus conducted by the RHS at Wisley. Out of 135 entries only three were given this award, the others being the commercial garden polyanthus strains of Crescendo and Rainbow.

The garden polyanthus

It is generally agreed that the polyanthus arose from a cross between the primrose and cowslip, probably between garden forms rather than wild plants. Primrose flowers are borne on separate stalks, while those of the cowslip, oxlip and polyanthus are borne together at the top of a common stalk or 'scape'. The earliest illustration of a polyanthus appeared in the 1687 catalogue of the Botanic Garden of Leiden University in The Netherlands. The plant shown in the catalogue has small, red flowers, which appear to be of jack-in-the-green form. By the 1670s, the name 'polyanthus', derived from the Greek polyanthos, meaning 'many-flowered', was in general use, describing a plant that was neither a primrose nor cowslip. It was not, however, until the late 19th century that the polyanthus began to develop into the plant we know so well today. At this time, the famous gardener Gertrude Jekyll

Crescendo polyanthus

introduced her 'Munstead' strain of whites and yellows, and within a few years many new strains were being sold by well-known firms like Waterers, Carters, Toogoods, Suttons, Blackmore & Langdon and others. Alas many of these companies no longer exist and fewer polyanthus strains are available today. From America Florence Bellis of the Barnhaven Nursery and Frank Reinelt, originator of the 'Pacific' polyanthus, had an enormous worldwide influence, which is still very prevalent today.

It has been suggested that the relative decline of the polyanthus is due to the need of the pot plant trade for a shorter, more compact plant. This may be so but it is still a superb garden plant, and not just for bedding purposes. The RHS conducted an invited seed

Barnhaven 'Indian Reds'

overwintering trial of polyanthus during the winter of 1996–97. There were 135 entries and the excellent German strain of Crescendo, from Ernst Benary, was given the Award of Garden Merit, as was the East Anglian-based company Floranova for their Rainbow strain. Seed or plants of these strains are well worth searching out. For growing in pots, Barnhaven polyanthus are probably the best, being smaller more refined plants. The pick of them is undoubtedly the fabulous Cowichan strain, which make wonderful pot plants, but several other Barnhaven strains are also very good.

Commercial primroses

The polyanthus reached its peak in the 1950s and 1960s, just as commercial plant breeders began improving the primrose. 'Improving' is a controversial word as there are two schools of thought on this work: some people believe that the present-day developments represent 'the epitome of the plant breeders' art'; others are less complimentary, feeling that the charm and beauty of the original species and hybrids has been lost in a blizzard of huge garish flowers and coarse foliage on plants, many of which are considered half-hardy at best. However, it cannot be disputed that the general gardening public buy these modern primroses by the million every year. Among them are some fabulous plants and wonderful colours, one well-known strain being the unfortunately named 'Wanda' hybrids, with brilliant colours set off by bronze foliage. The competition between competing companies is intense and new strains are introduced and older ones improved with great regularity. Some exciting developments are planned and we await them with anticipation. Seed of many of these strains is also available.

Barnhaven March

CULTIVATION AND PROPAGATION

Primroses require a moist, well-drained, fertile soil, containing ample humus, and a partially shaded position. The ideal is that the plants are exposed to early morning sun but shaded for the remainder of the day. During high summer and dry periods they must be well watered and given top dressings of some form of humus. Whatever mulch is used, it should be well rotted or decayed, especially if it is some form of animal manure. Old recommendations included garden compost, hen manure mixed with peat, cow or horse manure, mushroom compost, leaf mould, sedge peat, spent hops, seaweed and even chaff. Today we have substitutes, although they are not necessarily better. One point about manures deserves mention. Present day enthusiasts are frequently frustrated when they read of the apparent ease with which primroses were grown in past centuries. Some have studied the old writings avidly in order to discover how this was achieved. With present-day environmental and population changes, this is almost certainly a wasted effort but one factor may be relevant. Up until the mid-20th century the main mode of transport was the horse. Horses far outnumbered cattle and horse manure was available in large quantities. It was the primary source of manure for gardens, especially for the less well off, so it can be assumed that far more primroses received this form of nourishment. While the motor vehicle has now replaced the horse, there is still a large equine population, kept for recreational purposes. Riding schools and livery yards often give manure away free – you simply have to collect it. The essential point is that this material must be well rotted. If not, it should be stored in a suitable place and/or compost bin protected from the elements, to avoid the leaching of nutrients, until it is ready for use. Horse manure is also available in the form of mushroom compost. This contains chalk but as primroses are not recognized lime haters, it can be very useful.

In past literature it is not uncommon to come across 'disasters', involving the loss of plants, often in considerable numbers. This is despite primroses being 'amongst the easiest plants to grow' Genders (1958). Hecker (1971) states 'Our native primroses and cowslips can be found ... in almost any kind of soil, in sun or shade ... unaffected by the coldest of winters'. He continues by saying the largest plants are to be found in the West Country and Ireland, areas that are comparatively mild and have a high rainfall. More recently Barbara Shaw (1991) writes 'Primroses ... are not difficult plants'. However Graham Rice, in an interesting chapter on primroses in his book *Herbaceous Perennials* (1995), discusses the difficulties of growing named clones, particularly doubles. He blames drought and vine weevil as 'the two reasons that primrose-growing in Britain has been in a state of crisis'. While I agree in principal with these observations, I think there are also other factors involved.

Modern conditions are very different from those in the past. Many writers tell of growing their primroses under the shade of trees in apple orchards, a preferred site in the distant past. Shady banks and ditch gardens are other quoted habitats. My father, in private service in the late 1930s, grew primroses, including many named singles and some doubles, on the banks of a stream. These conditions still exist today for a few, but the majority of interested gardeners and enthusiasts have to make do with less ideal situations. We are also unaware of what effect atmospheric changes have had on the plants. In an appendix to Sacheverll Sitwell's *Old Fashioned Flowers* (1939), Mrs Eda Hume, a prolific writer on primroses, blames the loss of her plants on moving to a 'small town garden [with] buses passing, leaving exhaust fumes and petrol smells, and road dust'. While this is not scientific observation, one wonders what she would have made of present-day conditions!

These comments refer mainly to named clones and doubles, rather than the modern, commercially available seed-raised plants. With rare exceptions, these modern primroses and polyanthus are not intended to be maintained by division, but replaced annually by newly purchased plants. Seedling vigour provides a good show for a year or two, even in less than perfect conditions, and the plants should be grown in a similar way to garden polyanthus (p.28). Occasionally a special plant will arise that has the elusive ingredient of longevity and may be kept alive for several years or longer. A relative of mine, who lives in the Tyne Valley near Newcastle, has a particular large, yellow-flowered polyanthus that he has divided and maintained for some years. This practice is particularly relevant in the case of Barnhaven seed-raised plants, some of which are exceptionally attractive.

SINGLE PRIMROSES

If conditions are suitable – a mature garden with good shade and fertile soil – the orthodox methods work well for single primroses. The soil must be well-drained containing plenty of humus, ideally well-decayed farmyard or horse manure that has been kept under cover, and half-rotted leafmould. The bed should be well dug to a depth of at least 30cm (12in), by the old method of double digging if a spade is used. Incorporate the manure in the bottom layer with the leafmould in the top 50–75mm (2–3in). The leafmould should ideally consist of beech or oak leaves. Collect these in the autumn and put them, slightly damp, into black plastic binliners. Tie the bags and make a few holes in them, then place them in a garage or shed for 9–12 months. After this time, put the partially decomposed leaves through a shredder. The resulting shredded leaves are perfect for either composts or the top-dressing of precious plants. If either manure or leaves are not available then try one or more of the commercially available replacements on sale at garden centres.

Shade

Shade is another essential element, especially broken not dense shade. Small deciduous trees or shrubs are good shade providers. Primroses flower when branches are bare: leaves start appearing in late spring and so shade the primroses during the hot summer months. They also provide a mulch and humus with their autumn leaf fall. This is what happens in nature. In more open positions, growing the primroses among herbaceous plants or even annuals can serve the same purpose.

DOUBLE PRIMROSES

In general, the same remarks apply as for the single primrose, except that doubles require more care. While large numbers were grown in the 18th, 19th and early part of the 20th centuries, cultivation has always been troublesome. The exception to this seems to have been the common white, yellow and lilac varieties. In the 1880s *The Gardener's Chronicle* often referred to the diffculties of cultivating these plants. However, there have always been those gardeners who have claimed they are 'easy'. Major Taylor of Glazeley Gardens was one such champion and was certainly successful for a time, growing thousands in a field and putting on large displays at RHS and NAPS shows in the 1950s. He dressed his field with chaff (the rotted remains of straw) because the local farmer

Double primrose
'Ken Dearman'

would not part with his manure but was happy to supply the chaff. The then editor of the NAPS (Northern) yearbook, the irascible Thomas Meek, grumpily wrote that he would believe double primroses were easy plants when Major Taylor came and grew them in his garden.

Another successful grower, William Holt, in Somerset, recommended regular splitting and replanting while cautioning against too small divisions. He grew his plants in shade tunnels in which the soil had been specially prepared, using the local sedge peat rather than fibrous mossy peat. Bone meal and Phostrogen were used to dress the beds, and insecticides and fungicides were sprayed on a regular basis. Holt was also adamant that they should never be allowed to dry out.

Double primroses are prone to rot in the centre, possibly due to the large number of flowers they produce, so spent flowers should be removed and a careful watch kept for signs of rot. Finally, they are gross feeders and need a richer soil than singles. Regular feeding is beneficial using one or more of the many high potash formulations on the market.

GOLD-LACED POLYANTHUS

As far as cultivation of the gold-laced polyanthus is concerned we can forget the old growers nostrums and summarize the main points. Gold-laced are not as robust as garden polyanthus. They are smaller with softer foliage. Grow them as you would the choicer primroses, protecting them from frost and east winds especially in harsher climes. They can also be grown in pots, although some people consider this an anathema. Pot culture is similar to that described for primroses (p.28).

GARDEN POLYANTHUS

Garden polyanthus are easy to grow and tolerate a wide range of conditions. This refers to seed-raised plants, which are relatively short-lived, surviving two to three years at most before being discarded. Bedding polyanthus are normally replaced after flowering; selected plants, especially of the Barnhaven strains, may be divided and maintained for longer but this is not done in general. They are easy to raise from seed and some strains can also be purchased as small plants ready for planting. The seedlings or purchased plants must not be allowed to suffer from lack of moisture in summer as this is often fatal. When large enough, they may be planted out from early September onwards; in milder climates planting out can take place as late as December.

Good soil preparation will give the best results but often a good display results even in less than ideal conditions. If a moist soil can be maintained, an open position in full sun gives excellent results. In semi-shade plants grow larger but may flower with less freedom. Soil fertility is important, as is a mulch, worked under the leaves and around the crown in March.

It is normal practice to grow polyanthus as bedding plants either in mixed colours or individual shades. When he was in private service, my father grew hundreds of polyanthus every year. Usually they were arranged in mixed colours, but the blue shades were always grown separately. An alternative method is to plant small groups of from five to nine plants of a similar colour, in a partially shaded, front-of-border position, among small, deciduous shrubs and herbaceous plants.

GROWING IN POTS

Gold-laced polyanthus Kaye's Strain

While not ideal, pot culture can achieve excellent results and provide much pleasure. The normal view is that long-term pot culture is unsuitable for primroses and polyanthus, and plants in pots will soon deteriorate. This is not altogether true, although some variation in the behaviour of individual plants does occur. Some gardens, especially modern ones, are too small with unsuitable soil or a poor aspect for growing them in beds. In these instances, primroses are best grown in pots in a small greenhouse, cool conservatory or frame. The large-flowered pot strains, as well as named varieties and home-raised plants can make excellent pot plants and provide masses of bloom in late winter and spring.

The plants can be grown in plastic pots in various sizes. Small plants start off in 9–10cm (3 $\frac{1}{2}$–4in) pots and can then be potted into a larger size when the roots start coming out of the drainage holes. I find that 12cm (5in) pots are mostly adequate except for the very large polyanthus, which are best grown in the garden. Some especially vigorous singles and doubles may need pots of up to 20cm (8in).

The compost – a modified John Innes-type is suitable – should be well-drained, fertile and contain a good supply of humus, such as fibrous peat, shredded leaves or composted pine bark. If pine

White jack-in-the-green

bark is used, it must be of a grade specially prepared for composts. Equally satisfactory are soilless composts; there are several reputable makes on the market and some include a small amount of soil as a back up. Obviously the plants will need feeding, a balanced or high potash fertilizer being most suitable. Seaweed or fish-meal fertilizers are also beneficial with soil-based composts.

With pot culture, plants need re-potting annually, September being a good time for this. The process is similar to that of auriculas, removing all the old soil and any dead roots, together with any necessary trimming of foliage. Water the plants well after re-potting and keep them cool and shaded. Take care with the watering and they should be re-established in three to four weeks.

PROPAGATION

Division

If primroses are happy, they will increase to form large clumps. If left, many have a tendency to die out in the centre and should be divided every two or, at most, three years. Those with *P. juliae* blood increase by stolons, which root as they spread. They are easy to divide, but *P. vulgaris* types make separate crowns that have to be gently (or firmly) teased apart to form new plants. There are no hard-and-fast rules about this. Obviously the plants should have more than one crown – hopefully several.

Propagation by Division

Weather conditions and location are other determining factors. In southern areas, early autumn is probably the best time to divide plants; never attempt it during hot, dry periods.

The process of division is straightforward and involves separating the new crowns from the old rootstock, which is then discarded. Some can literally be pulled apart while others, if the clumps are large and tough, need to be prised apart using two hand forks, back to back. A hand trowel can be used to carefully separate divisions while the plant is still in the ground. This is most likely to be done with *P. juliae*-type, spreading plants. The division can then be lifted with ample soil around the roots and when replanted will quickly settle in. Sometimes it may be necessary to separate rootstocks with a knife, but avoid this if possible.

When replanting, dust the cut surfaces with green or yellow sulphur. Some people recommend shortening the roots and twisting off the larger leaves. This is not essential, but taking care when dividing plants is a must. Another thing to avoid is splitting into too many divisions. Small divisions take longer to establish and often fail. Plant the divisions very firmly in freshly prepared soil and give them a thorough watering. They must not be allowed to dry out and need to be well established before winter with new root growth anchoring them into the ground. Sometimes rot will develop in the centre so treat them with a suitable fungicide as a preventative measure. A mulch is beneficial as long as it does not smother the plants.

MICROPROPAGATION OR TISSUE CULTURE

Very briefly, this process is a laboratory-based technique used to produce huge numbers of plants very rapidly. Primroses have been tissue cultured, notably a range of doubles, and the resultant plants are regularly on sale at garden centres and some nurseries. The most advanced method is known as meristem culture which produces virus-free stock. Meristems, the growth points of the plant, are often free of viruses, even in infected plants. Embryo flower-bud material can be used to produce similar virus-free plants. Unfortunately, tissue culture is not really within the province of amateur growers, although 'home' kits are available in the USA. Tissue-cultured primroses are initially very vigorous, having been cleansed of virus, but some growers claim that they are still diffcult to maintain over a longer period.

Raising from seed

Primroses and polyanthus are easy to raise from seed and the procedure is simple. The seed must be kept cool. Heat will not aid germination as a condition known as heat-induced dormancy occurs when 20°C (68°F) is exceeded.

Sow seed in early autumn soon after it ripens, or in late winter or early spring; either gives good results. Autumn germination varies from a few days to 3 to 4 weeks, while germination of spring sowings takes 2–7 weeks. Use a good quality soilless seed compost, such as peat or a peat substitute, with added perlite or vermiculite. Perlite or vermiculite is added to make pricking out more straightforward as the compost falls away from the roots more easily; in pure peat composts, entanglement of the roots usually results in damage. Several good seed or multi-purpose peat-based composts are available from garden centres. I much prefer these to loam-based seed composts.

Use small pots or trays filled to no more than 5mm ($\frac{1}{4}$in) from the top. Sow seed thinly and either leave uncovered or cover with a thin layer of vermiculite. It is often recommended that primrose seed be left uncovered as light is needed for germination. The problem with this is that mould may develop on the exposed seeds, especially if they are in a propagator. They are also more prone to drying out. Vermiculite or a fine grade of perlite will allow light to penetrate. After sowing, moisten the compost by standing the trays in 2.5–5cm (1–2in) of water (too much water will force dry or just damp compost from the tray). As the compost absorbs water, add more until it is moistened throughout. Finally, give a mist spray to ensure the vermiculite covering is fully moist, then place the trays in a cool place in the garden, not in the greenhouse. Protect them from the depredations of slugs and other pests: I put mine in a large tray and place this on bricks, so raising them 15cm (6in) or more off the ground. A clear cover with vents goes on the tray. If the trays are outside then protection has to be given from the rain.

When the seedlings appear – failure is rare – prick them out into cell trays or pots after the first true leaves develop. When they are sufficiently large, pot on into pots or larger cell trays – don't be too hasty with this. They can then be moved into their final positions, either in the garden or larger pots.

NAMED VARIETIES OF PRIMROSES AND POLYANTHUS

Listed below is a very small selection of what may be available. The *RHS Plant Finder*, published annually, is a good starting point. There are a large number of named plants in North America and Canada and some have found their way to Britain. Note that misnaming of plants is common!

'**Alejandra**' A Canadian plant introduced via tissue culture. Described as a 'Wanda-type hybrid with rich red flowers on to 15–20cm (6–8in) stems'.

'**Amy**' This is a 'Wanda' impostor, widely grown throughout the Pacific Northwest. It is a refined 'Wanda' with smaller leaves

Primula veris *'Katy McSparron'*

and brighter flowers, each having a white fleck.

'Barrowby Gem' A famous old polyanthus noted for its fragrance. Pin-eyed, clear, bright yellow flowers each with a small greenish centre.

'Dorothy' A miniature, pin-eyed polyanthus with some similarity to 'Lady Greer'. The flowers are larger with some pink in them.

'Guinevere' Usually referred to as 'Garryarde (sic) Guinevere', this is the famous Irish primrose/polyanthus with bronze foliage and dusky, pale pink flowers.

'Katy McSparron' A magnificent cowslip with fully double, rich yellow flowers. It has been tissue cultured.

'Kinlough Beauty' A miniature polyanthus bearing thrum-eyed, salmon-pink flowers with a cream stripe down each petal

'Saltford Breeze'

'Lady Greer' A delightful miniature polyanthus with typical *P. juliae* foliage of bottle-green, and small, fragrant, pale lemon-yellow, funnel-shaped flowers.

'Saltford Breeze' (P. Ward c1992). This seedling derived from *P. juliae* and a red Barnhaven jack-in-the-green, is a low-growing plant of creeping habit with rich magenta-red flowers.

'Schneekissen' ('Snowcushion') Raised in Germany in 1931, this is a small wide-spreading plant with

'Kinlough Beauty' typical *P. juliae* foliage and white, pin-eyed flowers.

'**Tomato Red**' A fairly modern variety bearing thrum-eyed flowers of an unusual shade of orange-red.

'**Wanda**' The most famous *P. juliae* hybrid and still the most common. Pin-eyed flowers of glaring magenta. Many other plants masquerade under this name.

Doubles

'**Alba Plena**' John Gerard's famous 'double white'. A plant of primrose habit with *P. vulgaris*-type leaves.

'**Alan Robb**' Pale orange flowers. Barnhaven seed.

'**Belle Watling**' Velvety red flowers. Barnhaven seed.

'**Blue Sapphire**' A mid-blue variety. Barnhaven seed.

'**Corporal Baxter**' A Barnhaven seed variety with scarlet flowers, shading to crimson.

'**Dawn Ansell**' A beautiful, large-flowered, white, jack-in-the-green double from Cecil Jones. This one provides some pollen.

'**Eugénie**' A lovely shade of light blue.

'**Lilian Harvey**' Bright cerise-pink flowers with a yellow centre.

'**Miss Indigo**' One of the best, a very free-flowering plant with dark bluish-purple flowers, laced with silver. Barnhaven seed.

'**Sue Jervis**' A dull pink primrose, said to have been discovered growing in a wood in Shropshire.

HYBRIDIZING

It is very rewarding to raise your own plants, and primroses and polyanthus are particularly suitable for hybridizing, although doubles are difficult. Primroses are divided into pin-eyed and thrum-eyed plants. The pin-eyed plant is the seed parent while the thrum-eyed plant is the pollinator. Both types can set seed, pin **x** pin and thrum **x** thrum are possible but not really recommended.

The procedure is to take pollen from the thrum plant and place it on the pin or stigma of the selected seed parent. Check that the pollen-bearing stamens are ripe by inspecting them with a magnifying glass; if ripe they have a fluffy appearance. The pin, or stigma, should have a moist appearance when similarly inspected. Plants are most receptive when the flowers are young and not fully open.

Various methods of transferring pollen can be used but I normally take the ripe stamens, held in fine tweezers, and carefully make direct contact with the pin. Alternatively, if an individual flower is used, the petals folded back and the stamens pressed against the pin. A soft brush or piece of folded tissue can also be used to transfer pollen. Whatever the method, it must be done carefully. To avoid contamination with unwanted pollen, plants should be isolated or covered with muslin or similar material; when doing the latter, take care not to damage the flowers.

Hybridizing of doubles is probably best left to experts. A pin-eyed single is selected as the seed parent and pollen from a double is transferred to it. Doubles do not set seed and most have little or no pollen; the flower has to be carefully dissected in the hope of finding some. The stamens, if present, are at or near the centre, attached to the lower part of the petals. Often

Hybridizing

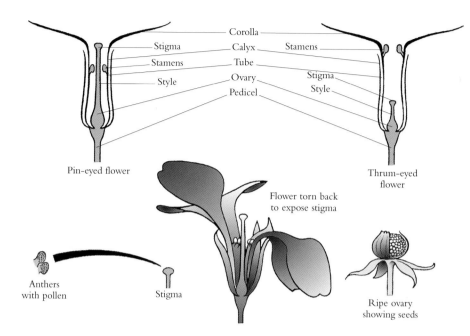

Pin-eyed flower

Thrum-eyed flower

Corolla — Calyx — Tube — Ovary — Pedicel

Stigma — Stamens — Style

Stamens — Stigma — Style

Flower torn back to expose stigma

Anthers with pollen

Stigma

Ripe ovary showing seeds

none are found; sometimes just one. If you are lucky several may be there but the stamens are not always ripe, refusing to burst. When ripe pollen is found, it is transferred to the stigma of the single parent and, if successful, the resulting seedlings will be single. They are known as the F1 generation. These seedlings must either be intercrossed or pollinated by another double, any double will do. The first method will produce up to 25 per cent doubles, the second up to 50 per cent. Success is not guaranteed and these ratios can vary – usually downwards. My preference is to pollinate the F1 seedlings with double pollen. To arrive at your own doubles takes three to four years but is very rewarding when it happens.

Gold-laced polyanthus require the same procedures as primroses and garden polyanthus. Although only thrum-eyed plants are allowed for exhibition, crosses produce both pins and thrums and indeed many of the pin-eyed plants are of excellent form. Both pin **x** thrum and thrum **x** thrum crosses are carried out by individual raisers.

THE AURICULAS

INTRODUCTION

Auriculas, like primroses, are also members of the genus *Primula*. The individual species of primula are classified into 37 sections with auriculas being members of section *Auricula*, which comprises 21 species confined to the mountains of central and southern Europe. Most are very similar but we are only concerned with the hybrid plants known as 'Florists' auriculas', which cover show, Alpine and doubles, and border or garden auriculas.

It is generally accepted that florists' auriculas are descended from a hybrid between *Primula auricula* and *P. hirsuta*, two species from the European Alps that first appeared in European gardens around the mid-16th century. Exactly how the exotic edged, striped and double forms arose is a mystery.

The first known illustration of an auricula was that made for the manuscript of *I Cinque Libri di Planti* written by P.A. Michiel, for some years director of the botanic garden at Padua, Italy in the 16th century. A printed edition of this was published in 1940. Probably the first illustration of an edged auricula is in the painting *Portrait of Martha Rodes* by C. Steele (1750). This was reproduced in a wonderful little book called *Florists' Flowers and Societies* by the late Ruth Duthie, which is out of print but well worth searching for.

One of the many myths that has persisted about auriculas is that they were introduced into England by Flemish weavers fleeing religious persecution in the 1570s. However, at that time, these plants were still novelties and were grown only by the rich. Therefore, it is more probable that they arrived, as did most other flowers, by interchange between leading Continental and English plantsmen. The writings of Gerard and Parkinson indicate this was common. In England, John Gerard knew a few varieties in 1597 and by 1629 John Parkinson was describing a much greater number. During the 17th, 18th and 19th centuries, growing auriculas became a major craze, with both the rich, or rather their gardeners, and humbler folk, cultivating them in great variety and numbers.

In the late 18th and early 19th centuries a large number of what were termed 'Florists' Societies' were formed. Today a florist is someone who sells flowers from a shop but in the original context it was 'one who attempts to grow flowers to perfection'. Among the many florists' flowers were the auricula and the gold-laced polyanthus, initially referred to only as 'polyanthus'. With the auricula's development into a florists' flower came strict rules and standards for its appearance, not without considerable acrimony between the leading lights of the day, including James Maddock and George Glenny. Towards the end of the 19th century a movement developed against what were termed 'artificial flowers' and florists' flowers lost popularity, some disappearing completely. The auricula, however, retained a loyal following, especially in the North of England, although stripes vanished and doubles became exceedingly rare. A National Auricula Society was formed in 1862 only to cease in 1865. In 1872 it was resurrected in Middleton by a group of Lancastrian and Yorkshire enthusiasts. A Southern section followed in 1876, with a show at the Crystal Palace and, somewhat later, in 1900, a Midland section was formed. These three groups refer to themselves as 'sections' of the National Auricula and Primula Society (NAPS), the titles later amended to include primulas. The use of the word section has caused much confusion over the years, leading people to think there is one society. In reality they are three quite independent groups, best described as having a common purpose.

The auricula is a plant with a fascinating history, one aspect of interest to garden historians being the so-called 'auricula theatre', an example of which was discovered a few years ago in

Parts of an Auricula

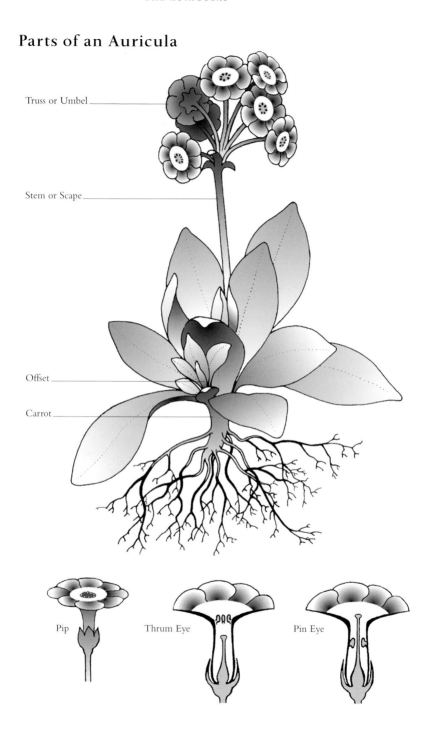

Truss or Umbel

Stem or Scape

Offset

Carrot

Pip

Thrum Eye

Pin Eye

Types of Auriculas

Self — One Colur unshaded

Edged — Paste, Tube, Edge, Body Colour — Four bands of equal weight

Striped — Stripes radial clearly defined

Green Edge — No meals on petals

Grey Edge — Light meals on petals

White Edge — Heavy meals on petals

Standard Alpine

Laced Alpine

Self Alpine

Two forms of Double Auricula

Border Auricula

the grounds of Calke Abbey in Derbyshire. This is the largest known still surviving, also intended for the exhibition of carnations. The structure is over 5.5 m (17 ft) wide and 1.5 m (5 ft) deep, and is some 200 yards from the Physick garden where the plants were grown. It has been restored and is used once more to display auriculas during the flowering season.

Although suffering a series of setbacks, notably during the two world wars, the auricula is now in a stronger position than at any other time. Stripes have been resurrected and doubles have become numerous. At present, the different types grown comprise show, Alpine (a capital A distinguishes them from alpine plants), double and border auriculas. Show types include green- and grey-edged, selfs, stripes and fancies. Alpines are either gold-centres or light-centres.

Auricula growers of the past had a mixed reputation, many being considered somewhat eccentric – indeed fanatical – in the way they grew the flowers. There are even authenticated reports of auriculas and gold-laced polyanthus being carried in funeral processions and interred with their late owners. Modern-day growers, while just as enthusiastic, are quite normal and often have wider plant interests. The societies, which are primarily responsible for the survival and current strength of the auricula, are thriving and the future looks bright.

'Brasso' yellow self show auricula

TYPES OF AURICULA

Auriculas are small herbaceous plants with one or more whorls or 'crowns' of leaves. These grow at the top of a short stout rhizome, called the carrot, from which the roots emerge. The roots are long and thong-like with finer feeding roots growing from them. New plantlets, or offsets, arise from the main carrot. They develop their own root system and can then be removed, usually during annual re-potting, and potted up separately.

Show, Alpine and double auriculas are normally grown year-round in small clay or plastic pots, in an unheated greenhouse or cold frame, with only the border types cultivated in the open garden. Some of the Alpine and double varieties will grow well, in well-drained, fertile soil in a suitable position outdoors, but most do not thrive under such conditions, especially the show varieties.

SHOW AURICULAS

Show auriculas are considered to be the aristocrats of the auricula

'Oakes Blue' blue self show auricula

world and have a ring of dense farina (a white powder or paste) around the eye of the flower. Most also have a dense covering on the leaves. The farina is the main difference between show auriculas and Alpines and doubles. Traces are sometimes visible on some Alpine varieties, disqualifying them for exhibition. Some border varieties have it and some do not. In the borders, attempts have been made to split the classification into 'garden' and 'border' types, depending on the presence of farina on either the leaves or flowers. Some doubles do have traces of paste but it

Green show Prague

is generally hidden by the double petals and often more obvious on the back of the pips (see illustration).

As the farina is easily spoiled by a single drop of rain, it has been normal practice to grow show auriculas under cover, and at the beginning of the 20th century only show auriculas were allowed on the show bench, hence the name.

Selfs and edges

Show auriculas are sub-divided into selfs and edged varieties. Selfs are all one colour. The edged varieties are unique in that the flowers or pips, including most stripes, have an outside edge composed of leaf tissue, which may or may not have the farina bearing hairs on it. If not, they are known as green-edged. If a smattering of farina masks the green, the result is a grey-edge, while a denser covering is called a white-edge.

Self-coloured auriculas are mostly red, yellow, auricula blue, a unique shade, and a very dark red, which can appear almost black. In recent years, many new colours have appeared, including brown and very pale yellows. The flower must be of a uniform even colour with no shading.

Edged flowers are quite remarkable. Green-edged is the most sought after as there are few green flowers in nature, and those that exist don't have the striking beauty of the auricula. In common with other show types, the flower has a circular golden tube, surrounded by a band of pure white paste. However, in the edged flower there is a variation, known as the body or ground colour, which in modern varieties is almost always black. The body or ground colour occurs in a band, the inside edge of which is next to the paste. It is smooth and circular and feathers out towards the rim, but not as far – then comes the green edge.

Usually green-edges have the largest flowers; the grey-edges – a green edge with white farina obscuring the green colour – tend to have smaller flowers although not dramatically so.

'Orlando' grey-edged show auricula

The standards for a perfect flower, of interest primarily to exhibitors, are quite precise and define exactly the proportions of each of these parts in relation to the whole. While black, in reality a very dark red, has become the norm, this was not always so and some present-day hybridizers have been working to introduce varieties with other body colours. Varieties that don't meet these precise requirements have, in the past, been relegated to what is termed the 'fancy' class, frowned on by more orthodox growers but liked by those with more catholic tastes. To some extent, the fancies are being replaced by the increasing number of striped auriculas that have made great strides in recent years.

Stripes

Stripes died out sometime in the 1800s but were re-introduced after a 25-year dedicated effort, commencing in about 1970, by an amateur enthusiast, Allan Hawkes of Rabley Heath in Hertfordshire. Since then, inspired by Allan and often assisted

'Monmouth Star'
striped show auricula

by gifts of plants and seeds, others, notably Derek Parsons of Monmouth, have been raising many more. Each year, new varieties with even more striking markings and new colour combinations appear. Self-pollinating or 'selfing' of some of these striped plants has also produced a possible new breakthrough, flowers without striping but with a picotee edge.

So far it has not proved possible to produce plants with the shape or form of the best edged varieties and some think this will prove impossible due to the genetics of the plant. However, not all devotees agree with this statement and many continue to strive for improvement.

'Wye Hen' striped
show auricula

'Bolero' gold-centre Alpine auricula

ALPINE AURICULAS

To many people Alpine auriculas are the jewels of the auricula world. Although clearly related to other types, they are quite distinct. It is thought they originated in the Low Countries during the early 18th century whereas the edged varieties were developed in England, hence the early descriptions of them as 'English Auriculas'.

There are two basic types of Alpine auricula: gold-centres and light-centres. The main difference is that the gold-centred variety has a lovely golden ground surrounding the tube while the light-centred variety is cream-coloured. There are variations, usually explained by the two types having been crossed together, but gold and cream are the norm. There is also a variation in colouring with the gold-centres generally being dark red, shading to bright red, or shades of brown, shading to gold. The light-centres are more subtle in colour, being shades of near blue, red becoming pink, or purple shading to mauve. In the past other types of Alpine – laced and selfs – were grown and some hybridists are working to re-introduce them. Laced flowers have an abrupt change of colour resulting in a picotee edge similar to pinks (*Dianthus*), while selfs are evenly coloured throughout without shading.

'Gold Seal' double auricula

DOUBLE AURICULAS

Almost certainly arising as mutations of the border or garden auriculas, doubles were among the very early novelties grown by the early florists and are mentioned in gardening books of the 17th century. John Rea described them in his *Flora* published in 1665, although paintings by Alexander Marshall, a noted artist, reveal that doubles, including striped, were being grown earlier than this. Plants changed hands at up to £20, an enormous sum in those days, but fell out of fashion with the rise of the show auricula in about 1750.

Unlike the stripes, however, doubles never became fully extinct. They remained very rare for the next 200 years and in his book *Auriculas* (1958), Roy Genders dismissed them in one paragraph, saying he had seen only two. Up until quite recently, and possibly still extant, there was a plant called 'Mrs Dargan', which, according to Miss W. F. Wynne, writing about 50 years ago, was the last survivor of a 'greatly admired section of striped auriculas'. She also records that 'when properly grown, the blossom is double ... Regrettably it often blossoms single or with only one or two double flowers in the truss.' This plant has been used by some modern hybridizers in attempts to raise both single and double stripes.

'Fantasia' double auricula

Around the early 1960s American enthusiasts, notably Ralph Balcom and Mrs Denna Snuffer, working with plants that had produced extra petals spontaneously, produced doubles in the F2 generation. Soon plants and seed arrived in England and the renaissance began, initially with Ken Gould and Dr Lester Smith. Barnhaven began producing double seed, and from this seed several good doubles were named, indeed some are still flourishing. Later, the Barnhaven strain was improved when Jared Sinclair, the proprietor of Barnhaven, by now located in Cumbria, was given a number of new doubles by Hal Cohen, a prominent member of the Midland Section of NAPS. These were crossed with the Barnhaven plants, bringing about a noticeable improvement. Since then several other enthusiasts have taken up the task and increasing numbers of doubles, in a variety of forms and colours, appear annually at NAPS flower shows. New clearer colours, principally reds and blues are being developed and the first all new striped doubles have appeared. Prior to this the colours were mostly buffs, dull yellows and purples, although some bright yellows have been raised.

BORDER AURICULAS

The most modest and best-known type of auricula is the border or garden auricula. Some of the old names for them were dusty millers, recklasses and ricklers. They were the original auriculas and it is likely that the other types developed from them, perhaps as mutations or sports. There are some plants with traces of farina on both flowers and foliage, indicating a relationship with show auriculas, while others are meal free. It has been mooted that plants with farina should be classified as 'border' while those without should be called 'garden' auriculas. However, not to put too fine a point on it, border auriculas have generally been treated in the past as the mongrels of the auricula world with no fixed standards, all the odd plants that do not fit in the other categories being lumped together in this group. Many of the lovers of these plants don't exhibit and, thus, are not bound by the rigidities of rules, enjoying the plants for what they are. Plants that are exhibited vary in size from quite small to a few that are huge, at least in comparison to the other auricula types; some are more properly described as European primula hybrids, while some of the named 'antiques' that still exist are vastly overrated and not worth growing, let alone expending the effort needed to obtain them. Having said this, distinctive plants that are not just poor versions of show and Alpine auriculas do exist and are well worth growing. Some are scented and much sought after.

The border auriculas have been much neglected with little attempt to improve them through hybridizing. The potential is certainly there, however, and more varieties have been appearing in recent years. As with other auriculas, almost all new plants come from amateur growers, with few available from the commercial sector. Commercial seed – usually labelled 'Alpine Auriculas' – produces plants that are generally sub-standard although it is always possible that something good might appear. Sometimes distinctive plants are spotted growing in someone's garden or they appear on the show bench. If the owner can be persuaded to part with a piece then you are in business!

Traditionally border auriculas are grown in a position that gives them shade from the midday sun. They can be grown in full sun, if well watered during dry periods, but prefer a well-drained, open site, naturally shaded during the hottest part of the day. Good drainage is essential, especially during wet periods. Being alpine plants in origin, they are not out of place on large rock gardens, while raised beds, with specially prepared soil, are another option.

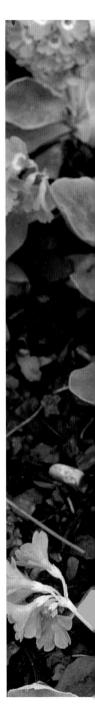

Border or garden auriculas

CULTIVATION AND PROPAGATION

Auriculas are hardy perennials and endure severe weather without difficulty. They may be grown in the open, but florists' auriculas are almost always grown in pots, under glass during winter and spring to protect the flowers and foliage from wind and rain. Show auriculas, especially those with a heavy farina, are very susceptible to weather damage as one drop of rain can mark the foliage or ruin the flowers. Bees are another problem, especially the large bumblebees which are attracted to the flowers and ruin the paste during their visits. If you wish to exhibit plants, bees must be excluded from the greenhouse.

The best way to grow show auriculas is in an open structure, ideally a well-ventilated greenhouse. Alpine houses used by specialist growers of alpine plants are the best choice. These have continuous ventilation along both sides and under the roof eaves. Some also have bottom ventilators, controlled by sliding wooden or metal panels. The snag is they are very expensive. Greenhouses in general seem to have become expensive, but it is wise to buy the largest model that finances allow. Often extra vents will be provided for a small additional cost. The auricula, which does not need heat, must be kept as cool as possible. Other structures can be utilized and many growers have shown considerable ingenuity in this respect. The key points are that plants must be protected from wind and rain (and bees) and kept in a cool and moist atmosphere during the hotter months. Greenhouses must be shaded during the hot summer months: in his 1934 lecture to the RHS, James Douglas of Great Bookham stated that 'using a medium fabric, we shade between 11am and 5pm (new time) from 1 April to 1 September'. Modern growers would agree with this although Douglas was located in the south so dates might vary slightly elsewhere.

COMPOSTS

Show auriculas are not fussy plants and grow well in a range of mixtures, with good drainage being probably the most important single factor contributing to success. The famous 'old growers' used a variety of homemade mixtures, including some that were thoroughly obnoxious, probably causing more harm than good. There are three basic choices. The first is the conventional one, although not practised by many today, of mixing your own loam-based compost. I did this in my early years of growing auriculas and obtained very good results. I think if you have the time and can obtain good quality raw materials – loam, leafmould (half-rotted leaves) and really sharp grit – then this is best. For the majority, however, this is not practical so the alternatives are a good quality, freshly made John Innes No.2 or No.3 loam-based compost or one of the many soilless composts available through garden centres. The problem with John Innes composts is the difficulty in obtaining really well made versions. Even if a good John Innes is obtained, it is still best modified with additional grit and humus to make it more open. There is a wide range of soilless composts, some are peat-based and others contain peat substitutes. One or two also include a small amount of soil.

Pots

Auriculas are grown successfully both in clay and plastic pots. Only two sizes of pot are required 7cm (3in) and 9cm (3½in). In my experience, show auriculas, which are slow-growing plants, do best in clay pots, preferably the long-tom variety, which is deeper than normal. The reason the long-tom is used is due to the tendency of some varieties to grow out of the pot: the carrot or stem elongates and may be 5cm (2in) or so above soil level. Other growers feel these special designs are unnecessary and many have now opted for plastic pots. They have advantages being much cheaper, lighter and easier to clean, but their disadvantages are that they are too shallow, have very thin sides and must be watered more carefully. Soilless composts are better suited to plastic pots: don't attempt to combine clay pots and peat-based composts. Some people use a soil compost and plastic pots with good results. Alpine and double auriculas are more vigorous than show types and will do well in plastic pots.

REPOTTING

This is an annual event with auricula growers. It provides the plants with a fresh supply of compost, allows inspection of the roots and carrot or stem, and enables offsets to be removed more easily.

Two periods are preferred for carrying out repotting, which is time-consuming if done properly. One is immediately after flowering in late May, the other mid- to late August, running into early September. In the south the later date is preferable. There are arguments for and against both periods, but it is a fact that the slow-growing auricula takes a while to re-establish itself after repotting. If it is done in May and a hot dry spell follows, the plants are very vulnerable to root and carrot rot.

The actual process must be done carefully to avoid losses. Allow the plants to become fairly dry so the soil is easily removed. Carefully knock them out of the pots – hold the pot upside down and tap it on the bench without breaking it (with plastic pots, squeeze the sides first). Most of the soil can be removed

Cutting back the carrot

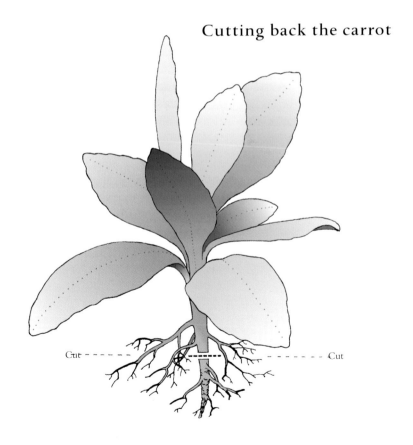

Cut - - - - - - - - - - - - - Cut

by gentle pressure and shaking. Remove any rooted offsets, together with dead and unhealthy looking roots. Examine the carrot for signs of decay and shorten it if it is very long. Use a sharp knife or scalpel for this operation, sterilizing it for each plant. Sterilize by immersing the blade in a diluted, fairly strong, solution of Jeyes fluid then cleaning it thoroughly (substances like this need careful handling, there are also other sterilants, household disinfectants for example). Wounds can be treated with flowers of sulphur or powdered charcoal. In general clay pots are 'crocked' before the plant is repotted (a few broken pieces of pot are put over the hole in the base to assist drainage); plastic pots have more drainage holes but despite this some growers still put in a bottom layer of crocks, or

Types of offset

alternatives like perlag or hortag granules. In clays plants should be firmly potted with fresh compost, finger pressure is sufficient. In plastic pots, lightly firm the compost, whether soil-based or soilless. Water well by standing the pots in water – up to two-thirds depth for clays, less for plastics. Soilless composts, especially peat, can take up enormous volumes of water so be very careful when watering this type of compost. Finally, place the plants in a cool shady place, giving them a mist spray on warm evenings. Take care not to water again unless you are certain it is necessary. This applies for the next month or so until the new roots develop.

Propagation

Auriculas are hybrids and are multiplied by the taking of offsets – small plantlets that grow from the stem or carrot. This is done when repotting and is the only way of increasing named clones other than tissue culture, which is not practical for the amateur. The number of offsets produced varies from one to four on most show auriculas, but can be considerably greater on some of the Alpines and doubles. Borders, being grown in the garden, are slightly different: they make clumps and are usually divided. It is preferable to take offsets with some roots. Most have a few and potted into small pots they grow away without difficulty. The Alpines and doubles are more vigorous and make large plants in a relatively short time. Show auriculas vary: some varieties take a while to mature, others are much faster. This is one reason why many desirable auriculas are always in short supply. When offsets are removed take care to cauterize any wounds on the carrot with powdered charcoal or flowers of sulphur.

Seasonal care

Spring

Whether the winter has been mild or not, new growth can commence as early as the end of January. The dull green of the fat central bud assumes a lighter, brighter hue and leaves begin to unfold. This is slow at first but then accelerates. Once growth is obvious, watering should be increased, ideally by immersion in 5–7cm (2–3in) of water. Don't overdo this, but from

February to May watering can be quite copious, as this is a period of quite rapid growth for what are otherwise slow-growing plants. By early March flower stems are rising fast and some, usually selfs, may even be in bloom. The peak flowering period is the latter half of April until the beginning of May. As with most plants, auriculas flower earliest in the south and up to two weeks later in the north. These are general rules and there are always exceptions: the auricula is a plant that likes to confound.

The overall treatment of plants during this period consists of keeping them well watered. At the beginning of March, a liquid feed can be given at half-strength; this is repeated two weeks later. It should be either a balanced feed or a high potash one. Increase spacing as the plants grow, especially those with mealed leaves. Finally, shade early in March or a little later in the north.

Summer

The summer months are the most dangerous for show, Alpine and double auriculas growing in pots. The plants must be kept as cool and well shaded as possible because heat together with too much water can be fatal.

When flowering is over, remove the flowerheads, except for those plants that have been pollinated. Allow the flower stem to wither and turn yellow after which it is easily plucked out.

June to August is one of the most crucial periods for these plants. After flowering, they enter a torpid stage when they do little more than look unhappy. Watering has to be done very carefully, bearing in mind that auriculas store water in the fleshy leaves and thick carrot and will stand being dry for a few days. Keep them well shaded and as cool as possible with a mist spray of water in the evening of hot days. Remove yellowed leaves, which, if ready, will come away with a gentle tug. Check the plants in the morning by testing the leaves. Just flick the leaf with your finger to see if it needs water (if the tip is slightly soft then water is needed). If the compost is moist and the leaves limp, this often indicates either root or carrot rot. In very hot weather, even heavily shaded plants will go limp, so take care. If in doubt, don't water!

Autumn

When re-potting and potting on are finished, ideally by early September, plants will begin settling into their new compost and making new growth. This is not as vigorous as the late spring period when the leaves reach their maximum size. Even so it is an important period and may determine the flowering performance in the following year. In October a feed may be given: a high potash fertilizer is best. In the absence of autumn frosts, use Chempak 0-10-10 (the N:P:K ratio), containing no nitrogen, to harden growth. Finally, take care when watering not to lodge any water in the heart of the plant, and remove yellowing leaves when they are ready.

Winter

Once the first frosts arrive, auriculas rapidly assume winter garb, a dismal-looking appearance. In severe winters the outer leaves die off and foliage is reduced to a fat central bud. With the recent run of very mild winters, this has become rare, and plants have remained quite leafy and often needing a little water. Otherwise little can be done other than removing dead leaves before botrytis sets in, and making sure water does not lodge in the crown. In frosty weather the plants go limp and it is not easy to tell whether water is needed or not. One method is to test the central bud, which if slightly soft indicates water is required. Don't water at all if temperatures are below freezing. Apart from the necessary overhead protection, auriculas are bone hardy and, providing they have not been grown too soft, will take cold and freezing weather in their stride. Finally, keep an eye for the commencement of new growth, which starts in winter, late January or early February. Remember the first day of spring is not until 21 March.

NAMED VARIETIES OF AURICULAS

There are a very large number of named auriculas in circulation – possibly over 2000. Unfortunately, many are of poor quality. Most have been raised by amateur gardeners who are members of the various NAPS societies. In the last 60 years, and even before, very little hybridizing has been attempted by commercial concerns. This is because the auricula is a slow-growing plant and even slower to increase, and therefore makes a poor commercial proposition. When mass production of show and other types of auricula was attempted via tissue culture a few years ago, it was only partially successful and a small range of tissue-cultured plants of mixed quality is sometimes available at garden centres and nurseries. A number of small specialist nurseries sell auriculas, the owners of most being members of one or more of the three NAPS societies. The better quality, named plants are always difficult to obtain. A stream of new seedlings, many subsequently named, are introduced annually at NAPS shows. As it can take several years or longer for individual plants to multiply into significant numbers, the difficulty in obtaining these latest varieties becomes obvious.

In recent years there has been increasing interest from non-specialist gardeners but there is rarely enough stock to supply the demand and, regrettably, this has led, in some instances, to inferior plants being offered for sale. It has been said that there are 'exhibition' varieties and 'commercial' varieties. In reality no such definition exists: plants are either good, bad or average.

It is unlikely that any commercial concern would have every plant listed below. The only way to obtain some of them is to join one or more of the NAPS groups and visit the shows or other events where plant sales occur. The hardest to obtain are the green-edges. They have always been scarce, increasing slowly, with many varieties fading away after a few years. Grey-edges are rather better and selfs even more so. Alpines and doubles are easier again and most increase rapidly, although there are exceptions. Striped auriculas are quite new and a large number of new varieties have been introduced in the last few years. Derek Parsons has been raising more than 1,000 striped seedlings annually for some years and has released close on 100 named varieties. This is already having a major effect on the availability of stripes. Nevertheless, it will take time for these plants to become more freely available. The following are only a small selection.

Show auriculas

Green-edged
'**Chloë**' (F. Buckley, 1957) First shown in London in 1967, 'Chloë' was the Premier green-edge for many years but is now showing signs of age. (Premiers are awarded to plants judged best in show in their particular category).At its peak it is a stately plant with a beautiful, well-proportioned, circular tube with no serrations.

'**Fleminghouse**' (J. Stant, 1967) Although often grown with a rather ragged tube 'Fleminghouse' rivalled 'Chloe' in popularity, especially in the North. It is suspected to be from green ✗ grey parentage. Many Premiers.

'**Prague**' (D. Hadfield, 1976). A fine plant produced by David Hadfield. This is a strong healthy grower that can produce a large flower truss. It is not perhaps of the finest quality but its combination of strong growth and reliable flowering has gained many awards including Premiers.

'**Roberto**' (R. Newton, 1969) A green ✗ grey cross, which Dr Newton believed produced a more vigorous plant. This is one of the best greens having won numerous Premier awards, but it is difficult to obtain.

'Roberto'
green-edged show
auricula

Grey-edged

'**Brookfield**' (P. Ward, 1979) A vigorous, untidy grower with one Premier award. Whitish grey with a nice round tube, this makes a good beginner's plant.

'**Clare**' (P. Ward, 1980) A good grower and reliable flowerer, but quite variable. At its best 'Clare' can be very good and has won several Premiers. Sometimes the tube is too large.

'**Grey Hawk**' (D. Hadfield, 1988) A very nice grey with a slightly dull tube. This has the desired 'leaden' look rather than veering towards white. Good proportions and reliable flowering have seen it awarded several Premiers, but it is not the most vigorous of plants.

'Clare' grey-edged show auricula

'**Iago**' (D. Hadfield, 1988) A plant with several similarities to 'Grey Hawk' but not considered quite as good. A reliable flowerer.

'**Margaret Martin**' (A. Martin, 1973) Since its introduction in 1974, this has been one of the most sought after auriculas. Although very successful, with many awards including Premiers, the magnificence of the original plant has never been equalled by its offspring.

'**Orlando**' (D. Hadfield, 1988) From the same cross as 'Iago' ('Grey Friar' x 'Stephen'), this is another excellent grey from David Hadfield. It has the same leaden look as 'Grey Hawk': in other words a true grey.

'**Sharman's Cross**' (P. Ward, 1976) A whitish grey, often shown as a 'white'. A plant of variable quality, it has performed quite well on the show bench.

Selfs

'April Moon' (T. Coop, 1988) A beautiful vigorous yellow self, fairly pale in colour but with large, well-formed pips. A good reliable grower.

'Barbarella' (P. Ward, 1980) A vigorous plant bearing a strong resemblance to its pollen parent 'Mikado'. The leaves are lightly covered in meal, offsets are produced freely and soon mature into large, flowering plants. A large truss of well-formed near black pips is produced.

'Brasso' (T. Coop, c1990) A bright yellow self with good form and vigour.

'Cheyenne' (P. Ward, 1971) This has been a leading red self for many years and it has excellent form. The foliage is not heavily mealed; the meal is prone to a yellowish tinge in late autumn and winter. The colour is a rather dark red and much brighter reds are now being raised. An excellent beginner's plant.

'Mikado' dark self show auricula

'Geronimo' (P. Ward, 1971) From the same cross as 'Cheyenne', and to all intents and purposes almost identical.

'Lemon Drop' (T. Coop, 1984) A reliable lemon-coloured self, producing small, neat pips on a large well-formed truss. Not as good as some other yellows but a vigorous grower, increasing rapidly.

'Limelight' (T. Coop, 1988) A beautiful pale greenish cream classed as 'any other colour'. A small plant with lightly mealed leaves, 'Limelight' is still scarce and may remain so for some time.

'Mikado' (W. Smith, 1906) An incredible plant, raised almost 100 years ago and still winning prizes. 'Mikado' has long, lanky leaves that flop over the sides of the pot. They are light green with serrated edges and with no meal. The pips are carried on a tall stem and at best are large, sumptuous and black. Sometimes they are smaller and more of a dark red as also occurs with its sibling 'Barbarella'.

'**Oakes Blue**' (D. Telford, l972). Good blue selfs are one of the rarities of the auricula world and this one from Derek Telford, more noted as a raiser of Alpine auriculas, is one of the very best. It is a small to medium-sized plant with narrow, well-mealed leaves. The pip is medium-sized and the nearest to true blue we have, although the flowers often appear shaded. Form is reasonable but in general blue selfs are inferior in this respect to both yellows and reds.

'**Royal Mail**' (B. Coop, 1994) A bright red self with excellent form. One of the newer sorts that have made an impact in recent years.

'**Scorcher**' (T. Coop, c1993) From the late Tim Coop, a bright, lighter red than 'Royal Mail' again with excellent form. Another winner from the Coop family.

'**Taffeta**' (T. Coop, c1993) Tim Coop specialized in raising unusual coloured selfs. He died in 2002 but his work is being carried forward by his son Brian. '**Taffeta**' is a pinkish shade and was introduced commercially by a specialist nursery in 2002.

Stripes

'**April Tiger**' (A. Hawkes, 1985) Mauve stripes on a grey-white ground. A vigorous and consistent plant.

'**Catherine Wheel**' (D. Parsons, 1996) Brown with bright gold stripes.

'Catherine Wheel'
striped show auricula

'Marion Tiger' (A. Hawkes, *c.*1986) Deep cherry-red with narrow, white stripes.

'May Tiger' (A. Hawkes, 1986) Variable colour but usually greyish stripes on a dark red ground. Apparently tissue-cultured plants are available.

'Monmouth Star' (D. Parsons, 1999) Red-brown with yellow stripes. One of the new varieties from Derek Parsons.

'Raleigh Stripe' (A. Hawkes, 1979) One of the earliest of Allan's seedlings, with wide red stripes on a yellow-buff ground.

'Royal Mail' red self
show auricula

'Regency Dandy' (D. Parsons, 1999) Reddish-brown with yellow stripes; lighter than 'Monmouth Star'.

'Taffeta' pink self
show auricula

'Starsand' (D. Parsons, 1997) This was the first of the blue-and-white striped varieties. Many more have now been raised.

'Wye Hen' (D. Parsons, 1996) Reddish-brown stripes on a greeny-grey background.

Fancies

'Fanfare' (T. Coop, 1993) One of many grey-edged plants with body colour other than black raised by Tim Coop. The red ground flashes to the edge, which classifies it as a 'fancy'.

'Hawkwood' (Douglas) Grey with a dark red body colour. This has been a reliable variety for many years. Possibly the nearest to normal show standards of any so-called fancy, although newer varieties are now appearing with different body colours and improved form.

'Rajah' (Douglas) Bright scarlet body colour with green-edge. Popular for nearly 30 years. The form is very rough.

'Star Wars' (T. Coop, c.1993) Another from the late Tim Coop of Harrogate who crossed a pin-eyed, purple-bodied seedling with another grey-edge. From this cross many greys with different body colours have been produced, some of them interesting plants.

'Sweet Pastures' (J. Ballard, 1957) After more than 40 years, this remains a popular variety. It is green-edged with a delicate yellow body colour.

Alpine auriculas

Gold-centres

'Andrea Julie' (D.L. Telford, 1972) A popular variety with large pips of a lighter shade of red than is normally seen. The flower stem can be on the short side unless well grown. An attractive reliable plant.

'**Applecross**' (D. Edwards, 1968) Well-shaded pips of a rich crimson on a tall stem. A popular exhibition variety.

'**Bolero**' (C.F. Hill, 1964) A superb variety, always scarce due to its reluctance to produce offsets. Medium-sized pip of copper-red, shaded to an unusual tone of light apricot-pink.

'**Galen**' (R. Cole, 1970) Large, very dark crimson pips, somewhat lacking in shading. Despite this fault 'Galen' is a popular plant with exhibitors, perhaps due to the contrast it provides in multiple classes.

'Starsand' striped show auricula

'Fanfare' fancy show auricula

'**Largo**' (A. Hawkes, 1969) Another superb variety, frequently of Premier quality. A reasonable grower that rarely produces offsets, so again always scarce.

'**Lee Paul**' (D. Telford, 1990) A newish variety with distinctive dark brown pips of a sombre shade. The plant must be shown in fresh condition otherwise the colour tends to change.

'Largo' gold-centre Alpine auricula

'John Wayne'

Nevertheless, a fine plant bred from the colour-break 'Sirius'.

'Prince John' (J. Douglas, 1916) Alpines are much longer lived than show auriculas and this is one example of an older variety. From the famous Great Bookham nursery, alas long closed, this plant is still vigorous and produces a good truss of medium-sized pips of a maroon shade, paling towards the edge.

Light-centres

'Adrian' (A. Delbridge, 1970) A robust-grower with neat pointed leaves. The medium-sized pips are dark violet, shading dramatically to light lilac. From the late Arthur Delbridge, a leading Midland raiser and exhibitor of Alpine auriculas.

'Argus' (J. Keen, 1887) The oldest extent variety, still winning prizes after more than 100 years! A unique colour of dark plum shading to beetroot. Colour and form can vary but at its best it is capable of Premier quality.

'John Wayne' (L. Bailey, 1979) An excellent plant, easily capable of being grown to Premier standard, indeed it has won several awards. The large pips are of a medium plum shade with a lighter edge and the small centre has a fretted tube.

'**Mark**' (D.L. Telford, 1972) A large plant producing fine trusses with good-sized pips. The bright pink colour and classical shading made it the leading light-centre for some years. This is one variety that has been grown in the garden, forming large clumps.

'Mark'

'**Sandra**' (H. Cohen, 1973) An unusual and rare colour in Alpines, this is a fine mauve shading lighter with a small, well-defined centre. It has won several Premiers.

Double auriculas

'**Camelot**' (A. Hawkes, 1967) A vigorous dark red, becoming more purple as the flower ages. Rather weak footstalks have difficulty in holding the full pips upright, unless the plant is well cultivated and grown in good light. Offsetting freely, this is another variety that grows well in the garden.

'**Doublet**' (A. Hawkes, 1975) A very full, dark red double, offsetting freely. Will succeed in the garden but again can have rather weak footstalks.

'Susannah' double auricula

'Fantasia' (K. Whorton, 1999) A wonderful example of one of the very new types of doubles that are being raised. Mulberry-red, flecked and streaked with white.

'Golden Chartreuse' (G. Black, c1970) Raised from Barnhaven seed and a lovely golden colour. Considered to have 'roughish' form for an exhibition variety but a winner nevertheless. A strong grower.

'Gold Seal' (K. Whorton, 1996) A superb bright yellow from a leading Northern raiser of double auriculas.

'Gwen Baker' (D. Salt, 1988) Named at one of the RHS Westminster shows by Derek Salt in honour of Gwen Baker a well-known grower and personality, and my co-author on *Auriculas*. A superb variety with large, well-formed pips of a pale yellow shade. Tissue-cultured plants are sometimes on sale at nurseries and garden centres.

'Jane Myers' (L. Bailey, 1970) Two similar auriculas masquerade under this name. Both are lovely plants of a pale yellow shade with classical doubling. They are known as 'Jane

Myers I' and 'Jane Myers II'. It was thought the 'I' had expired but plants reappeared after 'II' had been introduced. At least one of them, although a full double, has a stigma and will set seed.

'**Susannah**' (A. Hawkes, 1960) A pale lilac-pink with excellent doubling. A vigorous grower that offsets freely. Another plant that has been grown in the garden.

'**Trouble**' (D. Salt, c1988) A fine double with superb form but a controversial colour. No two people describe the colour alike: it is a mixture of yellow, pink and green. Tissue-cultured plants are sometimes on sale at garden centres and nurseries.

Border auriculas

'**Bellamy Pride**' (B. Walker, c1985) A lovely white-flowered truss over lightly mealed leaves. The plant is thrum-eyed and the flowers have a slight bluish tinge, giving them a 'frosty' look. Not a very large plant, this is often grown in a pot, rather than the garden.

'**Broadwell Gold**' Now an old variety, this was discovered growing in a garden in Broadwell by Joe Elliot of the famous alpine nursery. Big, frilled golden-yellow flowers are borne on long strong stems soon making a large clump.

'**Charles Rennie**' (P. Ward, 1992) A seedling from 'Kate Haywood', this is named after a deceased friend. A vigorous plant with large, rounded heads of well-shaped, pale pinkish beige pips.

'**Kate Haywood**' A strong-growing plant with narrow, pointed leaves that are pale green and very lightly mealed. The flowers, on a long stem, are pale creamy yellow, sometimes even described as white.

'**Mrs Harris**' A huge, large-flowered plant, originally found growing in a garden in Cheltenham. The flowers are pin-eyed and pale greenish-yellow. An identical plant was sold by a Scottish nursery as 'Rab Dalgleish'. Quite the largest border, in both leaf and flower size, but on the gross side.

'Paradise Yellow'
Clusters of rather tubular pips, thrum-eyed, and bright yellow over meal-free leaves. Not a large plant for a border auricula. Introduced by the Paradise Plant Nursery.

'Rusty Red' border auricula

'Rusty Red' (P. Bowen, c1995) A very unusual plant from Peter Bowen of Llanelli who has raised other excellent borders. This one is outstanding with bright, attractive, rusty red flowers with a stained eye.

RAISING NEW VARIETIES

From seed

The procedure for raising auriculas from seed is similar to that already described for primroses: sow seed in early autumn, as soon as it is ripe, or keep it in a sealed container in the fridge (not freezer) until late winter or early spring (for more information, see pp. 30-31). The main difference is that auricula seed, particularly that of show auriculas, is much slower both in germination and growth. On at least one occasion, however, my autumn-sown seed has germinated in a few days so it is not possible to be dogmatic about such things. Seed is also tiny so needs careful handling. From germination to flowering with show auriculas can take 18 months to two years, sometimes even longer. Alpines,

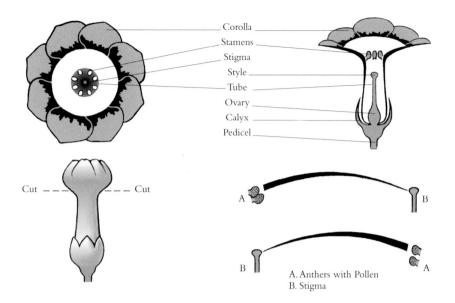

Corolla
Stamens
Stigma
Style
Tube
Ovary
Calyx
Pedicel

Cut – – – – – – Cut

A. Anthers with Pollen
B. Stigma

doubles and borders are more vigorous, and seedlings grow much faster.

HYBRIDIZING

To raise your own auricula seedlings is rewarding, but in the case of show auriculas can be particularly frustrating. Edged plants rarely produce other than small amounts of seed and frequently what appear to be healthy seed pods are empty. Experience is best gained with Alpines and perhaps borders before attempting to produce edges. Doubles also present a particular problem and are again best left until you have experience with other varieties.

With show auriculas the usual rule is self ✗ self, green-edge ✗ green-edge and grey-edge ✗ grey-edge. Stripes are a different matter; they are usually crossed together but sometimes with greens or greys. Alpines are gold-centre ✗ gold-centre and light-centre ✗ light-centre. Obviously these rules are not set in stone and those with an experimental bent may do what they like.

The process of crossing is complicated in that show auriculas and Alpines are all thrum-eyed. This is because pin-eyed plants are not accepted and over the centuries of auricula breeding have been virtually eliminated. I say 'virtually' as the odd one still occurs in crosses together with mid-pins – where the pin is on a level with the stamens. This means that the recognized cross is thrum x thrum, so that the flower of the designated seed parent must be removed to gain access to the stigma. The stigma is low down in the tube, and as the tube is narrow, it is a painstaking process to gain access and pollinate successfully. Usually the tube has to be opened slightly or cut down before the stigma is accessible. Otherwise the process of transferring pollen is the same as described for primroses. Tools required are a magnifying glass, fine tweezers and small, pointed scissors.

Crossing double auriculas brings the same difficulties as double primroses with three exceptions. First, generally more pollen seems to be available and, second, some doubles, surprisingly, have viable stigmas and can set seed (the well-known variety 'Jane Myers' is one such double). The third difference is that double auriculas are mostly vigorous and long-lived, producing offsets freely.

Results

Assuming one is successful, when the resulting seedlings flower what can one expect? Good new show auriculas are very hard to raise and the success rate is low. Nevertheless many do succeed, as shown by the large number of new varieties that appear at NAPS shows. However, most seedlings bear little or no resemblance to their parents and are usually much inferior. There are reasons for this, one being that the desired features are recessive, meaning they often disappear in the initial F1 cross. This is a complicated subject; it is suffice to say that most amateur hybridists – who are also responsible for nearly all new auricula introductions – are not scientifically inclined and simply follow their instincts.

Alpine auriculas are easier and the success rate is much higher. Seed is set more freely and the resultant seedlings more closely resemble the parents, although exhibition quality plants are still comparatively rare. Nevertheless, many new, quality seedlings have been introduced in recent years.

Many new doubles have been introduced and excellent new seedlings are exhibited annually. With doubles single, semi-double and double seedlings can arise from crosses; this is sometimes in the F1 generation – if a double is the seed parent – but otherwise doubling will not normally appear until the F2 generation. One problem is the extent of doubling, which can vary from flower to flower, single, semi-double and double flowers appearing on the same plant. Bright new colours, especially reds and blues, are being introduced and also striped doubles. Double crosses can set lots of seed and the resultant seedlings are vigorous.

Border auriculas are a mixture of pins and thrums, so the natural cross of pin x thrum is the norm. Seed sets easily, in large quantities, and the resultant seedlings are vigorous. As with all types of auricula, discretion should be practised in selecting and keeping only the best.

PESTS AND DISEASES

With one or two exceptions, auriculas and primroses are troubled by few problems. The auricula is a tough, hardy plant and when grown in the garden is virtually trouble free. Primroses are slightly more vulnerable but not excessively so. Show, Alpine and double auriculas are usually grown in greenhouses and here the main threat are the grubs of the vine weevil. When primroses are grown in pots, they also become very vulnerable to vine weevil, especially seedlings and smaller plants. Red spider mite is also a menace to both primulas and auriculas in pots. Auricula varieties with farina-covered foliage are particularly vulnerable, as are gold-laced polyanthus. For those who don't wish to use chemicals, biological controls using specific predators are available to combat most pests.

PESTS

Vine weevil

Vine weevil, principally the cream-coloured larvae that destroy the root system in late summer has been a scourge for some years. Biological control with pathogenic nematodes may be effective for those who don't want to use chemicals. Some commercial products that appear to give control are unavailable to amateur growers and as concern over pesticide use continues to grow, there is considerable uncertainty over the future availability of existing controls. However, the recent introduction of imidacloprid either as a compost drench or a pre-treated peat compost, seems to have eased the problem.

Another possible remedy is 'Armillatox', originally intended as a cure for honey fungus. Experiments with very diluted solutions have led to this product being given approval as a soil surface spray, which destroys the eggs and newly hatched grubs. The company that manufactures it only claims that treatment reduces the incidence of vine weevil; it will not eradicate existing larval infestations. The instruction leaflet issued with this product must be followed to the letter, otherwise damage to plants may result. We must hope that the adaptable vine weevil remains vulnerable to these products.

Life cycle of the vine weevil

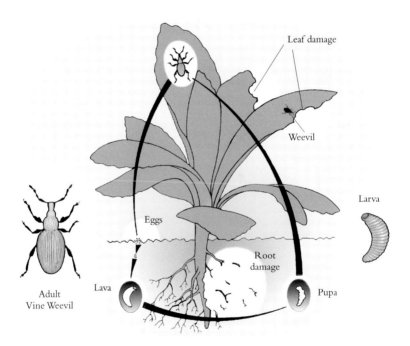

Leaf damage

Weevil

Larva

Eggs

Root damage

Adult Vine Weevil

Lava

Pupa

Red spider mite

Red spider mite is the worst pest of primroses in greenhouses. It will also attack garden plants. Nothing available to the amateur seems fully effective. Auriculas are attacked by red spider but when grown with primroses seem to be left alone. Insecticides containing *bifenthrin* initially seemed to work well. However, recent experience suggests that this pest may be growing resistant. One of the problems with red spider mites is that they cluster on the underside of the leaves, which makes spraying difficult. Immersing the plants in a solution in a bucket or tub is the only certain way of wetting the whole leaf area. Some sort of systemic insecticide is needed and the recent introduction of imidacloprid, in aerosol or spray form, may be effective, although the usual proviso about resistant strains appears on the label. Instructions for use must be followed to the letter with all insecticides and fungicides. An effective alternative to pesticides during late spring to early autumn, especially on greenhouse plants, is the predatory mite *Phytoseiulus persimilis*.

Root aphid

This pest is easily recognizable being covered with white, waxy wool – hence the common name of woolly root aphid. The aphids attack the roots and also appear above the soil around the neck of the plant when infestation is severe. Auriculas seem particularly prone to infestation, primroses less so. A severe infestation will debilitate the plant and may introduce viruses. Keep a close eye for signs of this pest and treat with a systemic insecticide, such as imidacloprid which should keep them at bay, although resistant strains may be a growing problem.

Greenfly

Greenfly appear in early spring but are a minor pest easily controlled by spraying with a recommended insecticide.

Whitefly

Whitefly can become a problem in greenhouses but treatment with imidacloprid or containing *bifenthrin* will control them. Biological controls are also available as an alternative treatment, such as the parasitic wasp *Encarsia formosa*.

Slugs and snails

These pests are a major problem in the garden but less so in greenhouses, especially where plants are grown on benches. Nevertheless, they do occur in greenhouses and can climb up to the plants, so vigilance is needed. Primroses are particularly prone to their ravages, auriculas less so. Slug pellets and other remedies are available but it is a battle the gardener rarely seems to win.

Fungus gnats

Also known as sciarid flies, these tiny black flies are common in greenhouses where they feed on decaying matter, and lay their eggs on adjacent soil. The larvae – small whitish translucent maggots with a black head – feed on any rotting vegetable matter available. Some auricula growers believe they also attack living plants but this is unlikely, unless rot is present. Plants growing in soilless compost may be more vulnerable, as are small seedlings. Control is by imidacloprid, watered onto the pots, while the adults can be reduced by spraying or by hanging yellow glue traps.

Birds

Small birds, especially sparrows and blue tits, may destroy the flower buds of primroses in the garden. Where this happens a simple solution is to stretch black cotton between two sticks, 5cm (2in) above the flowerbuds, along each row or group of plants. There are also sprays available that are supposed to make the buds unpalatable.

Diseases

Under glass, the most important disease attacking auriculas and primulas is grey mould or botrytis, caused by the ubiquitous fungus *Botrytis cinerea*. This fungus grows on dead plant material and the spores are therefore always present, if humidity is high enough to allow them to develop. It readily infects weakened or wounded tissue, particularly older, senescing leaves. Flowers are very susceptible and may be attacked even when undamaged. In addition to these well-known routes of entry, there is now good evidence from studies carried out at the University of Reading and Horticulture Research International, that the fungus may be seed-borne in primulas and develops in young plants in a symptomless fashion, only breaking out when plants are put under stress. In all cases, infected tissues turn brown and collapse and the fuzzy grey growth of the fungus and its spores rapidly appears if humidity is high.

Control is firstly by ensuring that plants are bought from a reputable, disease-free source, to avoid bringing infection into the greenhouse. All weakened, damaged, senescent and dead plant material should be removed promptly to reduce the availability of spores. It is very important to avoid high humidity by ensuring good ventilation. At present (2002), the fungicide carbendazim is available in two formulations for amateur gardeners for the control of botrytis on pot plants.

White mould (*Ramularia primulae*) has been recorded under glass. It causes blotching on the upper leaf surface, corresponding to a growth of white fungus on the lower surface. No fungicides are available to amateurs to control the problem and as with botrytis, avoidance of high humidity and prompt removal of infection is essential. The disease brown core caused by the fungus *Phytophthora primulae* is specific to primulas and causes a brown discolouration of internal tissues and collapse of the plant. It is spread in contaminated water or soil. There are no fungicidal controls for amateur gardeners.

In open ground, primulas may suffer from several leaf fungal leaf spots including white mould especially in wet conditions. These are common, especially on older leaves, but are not usually damaging and control is not warranted. Both brown core and several other non-specific fungal root pathogens also occur, causing poor growth or even collapse. There are no chemical treatments available to gardeners for these diseases and sites where they occur should not be replanted with primulas. A rust (*Puccinia primulae*) occurs, but is seldom damaging.

Rot

Auricula literature is filled with reports of loss of plants due to 'rot'. Two sorts affect auriculas: 'soft' rot attacks the crown; 'hard' rot or canker is often prevalent on older plants with thicker carrots. The best remedy is to ensure the conditions that the fungus thrives on do not arise. Good ventilation, an open porous compost and careful watering will keep it at bay. Regular replacement of older plants is also wise.

Viruses

Most viruses are transmitted by aphids or other sucking insects. Primroses are sometimes affected, usually by cucumber mosaic virus. Most of the very old varieties probably expired due to a build up of virus infection. Auriculas are rarely visibly affected by viruses although some older varieties do develop yellow streaks or blotches on the foliage. In 1980, research at Birmingham University Botanic Gardens established that at least two viruses were present in two of the older varieties tested. From the general behaviour of auriculas, it seems that a low level of virus infection can be tolerated but vigour is affected. Avoid spreading viruses by taking great care when re-potting or removing offsets with knives or scalpels, sterilizing them after each plant is treated. Pests that spread virus must be eliminated as quickly as possible and newly introduced plants screened to ensure virus is not introduced. Further research has been undertaken at Wye College in Kent.

Chlorosis

This denotes abnormal paling or yellowing of the leaves. It sometimes occurs in auriculas and primroses, usually due to iron deficiency but poor cultivation, often faulty watering or too high temperatures, can also cause it. If iron deficiency is the cause, watering with sequestene will remedy the problem.

GLOSSARY

Anther The part of the stamen that bears pollen, also called the thrum.

Callus A layer of cork-like tissue that seals wounds on a plant. Calluses are also formed at the base of offsets and the bottom of the carrot when it is cut.

Calyx Modified leaves, known individually as sepals, protecting the developing flower and later arranged round the base of each individual floret.

Carrot The rhizome or stem of an auricula.

Chlorophyll The green colouring in plants, necessary for photosynthesis.

Chlorosis A condition or disorder where chlorophyll is absent from the leaf margins, mostly caused by mineral deficiency, usually iron.

Crenate Having rounded teeth, usually describing the edges of leaves or the tube.

Cockled The common name for wavy or corrugated petals on auriculas.

Corolla The group of petals forming the flower.

Dominant One of two alternative characters in plants, visible in the offspring when both are inherited.

F1 Botanical shorthand for first filial generation, usually hybrids.

F2 As above except second filial generation; F1 hybrids crossed together.

Farina A white waxy powder common to many primulas and found on the leaves stems and flowers, often called 'meal' as it resembles flour.

Gene A unit in the chromosomes of an animal or plant, determining one character in the adult plant, such as a gene for doubling or a gene for virescence.

Genus A class or group of plants with common characteristics. Auriculas and primroses are members of the genus *Primula*.

Ground or body colour. The ring of colour next to the paste in the edged pip of an auricula.

Hybrid Offspring of two plants of different but related species, showing a diversity of features derived from both parents. Hybrids rarely breed true, the offspring showing further diversity.

Line breeding Breeding from related seedlings and recrossing the progeny of two parents, which has the effect of concentrating good genes but also bad ones.

Mutation An alteration in the genetic make-up of plants and animals, often called a 'sport'.

Ovary The part of a flower where fertilized seeds develop.

Paste The dense mass of farina surrounding the tube in the centre of an auricula flower.

Pedicel The stem or footstalk supporting each flower in a truss.

Peduncle The main stem or stalk of a truss of flowers.

Petal The individual coloured parts of the flower, forming the corolla.

Petaloid 'Resembling a petal'; describes parts of flowers changed from their normal function to resemble petals.

Pin-eyed A flower in which the style and stigma are visible in the centre or throat, above the stamens, which are lower down. In auriculas, other than borders, such a flower cannot be exhibited. See also thrum-eyed.

Pip Common name for the individual flower in an auricula truss.

Pistil The female parts of a flower, including the stigma, style and ovary.

Pollen The yellow powder made by the anthers, the male sex cells, transferred naturally or artificially to the female pistil, so fertilizing the seed.

Recessive gene An inherited character that is not apparent in the plant that inherits it but which may reappear in future generations.

Rhizome The part of the plant where food is stored and from where the roots and offsets arise, commonly called the carrot in auriculas.

Senescent Old, past its prime, moribund. Said of a stock plant which has been kept beyond its useful lifetime, or tree which is dying.

Species A collection of wild plants that breed true.

Stamen The male reproductive organ of the flower: a fine stalk or filament and the anther or pollen sacs; in auriculas and primroses the stamen is attached to the petals.

Stigma The pad at the top of the style, resembling the knob of a pin, that receives the pollen. (Also called the pin.)

Stolon A shoot that travels along the ground, rooting and producing a new plant at the tip.

Stoloniferous Producing stolons.

Style The hollow tube that joins the stigma and ovary and down which the pollen tubes grow to fertilize the seed.

Systemic A type of insecticide absorbed into the sap of a plant, rendering it poisonous to biting and sucking insects.

Thrum–eyed A flower in which the stamens are visible in the throat of the flower with the stigma or 'pin' usually lower down. See also pin-eyed.

Truss A flowerhead, correctly called a scape, the individual flower stems radiating out from the top of the main stem.

Tube The narrow channel down the centre of the flower which contains the sexual parts.

Virescence The abnormal greenness of petals, controlled by a gene and inherited by seedlings.

FURTHER INFORMATION

BOOKS

Those marked ★ are out of print but sometimes obtainable either from libraries or second-hand booksellers. *Primulas* by John Richard was available in the USA until quite recently.

Auriculas, Gwen Baker and Peter Ward (Batsford, 1995)★
Auriculas for Everyone, Mary Robinson (Guild of Master Craftsmen, 2000)
Auriculas, Roy Genders (John Gifford, 1958)★
The Auricula, R. Biffen (Cambridge and Garden Book Club, 1949)★
Auriculas and Primroses, W.R. Hecker (Batsford, 1971)★
The Book of Primroses, Barbara Shaw (David & Charles, 1991)★
Florists' Flowers and Societies, Ruth Duthie (Shire, 1988)★
Primroses and Polyanthus, Peter Ward (Batsford, 1997)
Primulas, John Richards (Batsford, 1993)★
Primulas of the British Isles, John Richards (Shire, 1989)

The NAPS (Midland and West) publishes a range of small booklets, primarily on auriculas, that are very informative. They are available to members and at NAPS (M & W) shows.

SOCIETIES

There are three National Auricula and Primula Societies, each calling itself a 'section' of the NAPS. Note that each is an independent society and must be joined individually.

National Auricula and Primula Society
Midland and West Section
Secretary: D.A.Tarver, 9 Church Street, Belton, Loughborough, Leicestershire, LE12 9UG.
Website: www.primulaandauriculas.co.uk
Northern Section
Secretary: D. Hadfield, 146 Queens Road, Cheadle Hulme, Cheshire, SK8 5HY.
Southern Section
Secretary: L. Wigley, 67 Warnham Court Road, Carshalton Beeches, Surrey, SM5 3ND.

American Primrose Society
Fred Graff, Treasurer, 2630W Viewmont Way W, Seattle, WA 98199, USA.

National Council for the Conservation of Plants and Gardens (NCCPG)
National Collections Scheme Under the auspices of the NCCPG a number of National Collections of various types of auriculas and primroses have been established. These include show, Alpine, border and double auriculas.
To obtain the latest information on collection holders contact: NCCPG, The Stable Courtyard, RHS Garden Wisley, Surrey GU3 6QP.
Tel: 01483 211465; Fax: 01483 212404

SUPPLIERS

Ashwood Nurseries,
Greensforge,
Kingswinford,
West Midlands, DY6 0AE
Tel: 01384 401996
Website: www.ashwood-nurseries.co.uk
Mail order only for Alpine auricula seed, also plants in season at the nursery. Gold-laced polyanthus plants.

Abriachan Gardens and Nursery,
Loch Ness Side,
Inverness, IV3 8LA
Tel: 01463 861232
Auriculas, single and double primroses.

Barnhaven Primroses,
11 Rue du Pont Blanc,
22310 Plestin les Greves,
France
Tel/Fax: 33 (0) 2 96 35 68 41
E-mail: barnhaven@wanadoo.fr
Website: www.barnhaven.com
Hand-pollinated primrose and polyanthus seed.

Cravens Nursery,
1 Fould's Terrace,
Bingley,
West Yorkshire, BD16 4LZ
Tel: 01274 561412
Auriculas and primroses.

Crescent Plants,
34 The Crescent,
Cradley Heath,
West Midlands, B64 7JS
Tel: 0121 550 2628; Website: www.auriculas.co.uk
Auriculas.

Drointon Auriculas,
Drointon House,
Stafford, ST18 0LX
Auriculas.

Field House Alpines,
Leake Road,
Gotham,
Nottinghamshire, NG11 0JN
Tel: 0115 9830 278
Fax: 0115 9831 468
E-mail: dlvwjw@field-house-alpines.fsbusiness.co.uk
Auriculas, primroses and polyanthus.

Garden Direct (Mail Order Division of Chempak),
Dept MO,
Unit 40 Hillgrove Business Park,
Nazeing Road, Nazeing, Essex, EN9 2BB
Tel: 01992 890550
Fax: 01992 890660
Order online: www.gardendirect.co.uk
E-mail:sales@chempak.co.uk
Wide range of difficult-to-obtain fertilizers (including 0-10-10), composts and other products.

Hillview Hardy Plants,
Worfield,
Nr. Bridgnorth,
Shropshire, WV15 5NT
Tel/Fax: 01746 716454
Auricula, single and double primroses.

Just Green,
Freepost Ang 10331,
Burnham on Crouch, CM0 8BF
Tel: 01621 785088
Fax: 01621 783800
Biological pest controls.

Lingen Nursery and Garden,
Lingen,
Nr. Bucknell,
Shropshire, SY7 0DY
Tel: 01544 267720
E-mail: kim&maggie@lingen.freeserve.co uk;
Website: www.lingennursery.co uk
Auriculas and primroses.

Martin Nest Nurseries,
Hemswell,
Gainsborough,
Lincolnshire, DN21 5UP
Tel: 01427 668369
Auriculas and primroses.

Pops Plants,
Pops Cottage,
Barford Lane,
Downton, Salisbury, SP5 3PZ
Tel: 01725 511421
E-mail: Pops@downton51.freeserve.co.uk
Auriculas.

Thompson & Morgan,
Poplar Lane,
Ipswich, Suffolk, IP8 3BU
Tel: 01473 688588
Fax: 01473 680199
E-mail: tmuk@thompson-morgan.com
Polyanthus and primrose seed.

Timpany Nurseries and Gardens,
Magheratimpany Road,
Ballynahinch,
County Down,
Northern Ireland, BT24 8PA
Tel/Fax: 00 (44) 028 97 562812

E-mail: timpany@alpines.freeserve.co.uk
Website: www.alpines.freeserve.co.uk
Auriculas.

White Cottage Alpines,
Sunnyside Nurseries,
Sigglesthorne,
East Yorkshire, HU11 5QL.
Tel/Fax: 01964 542692
Auriculas and primroses.

Many other nurseries offer a number of auricula and primrose cultivars, while seed of polyanthus and primroses is obtainable from most garden centres and mail order seed merchants.

ONLINE INFORMATION AND WEBSITES

www.wilkin94.fsnet.co.uk
A brilliant site with hundreds of photographs taken at NAPS and Alpine Garden Society shows.

www.wye.ic.ac.uk
'Florists auriculas at Wye' deals with the history of the auricula, along with modern research into micropropagation.

www.rhs.org.uk/plants/award_plants.asp
A complete list of plants given the RHS Award of Garden Merit.

INDEX

Acknowledgements:

Illustrations: David Tarver
Copy-editor: Jo Weeks
RHS editor: Simon Maughan
Proofreader: Rae Spencer-Jones
Index: Laura Hicks

The publisher would like to thank the following people for their kind permission to reproduce their photographs:

Cover image: The Garden Picture Library (Mark Bolton)
Scilla Edwards: pages 16, 20, 28, 30, 36, 42, 43, 44, 46 (top and bottom), 47 (top and bottom), 48, 62, 63, 64 (top and bottom), 65, 66 (top and bottom), 68 and 72
Peter Ward (all other pages)